Phonics Wonder

LEVEL 5

Double Letter Vowels

YSG Young & Son Global, Inc.

Contents

Lesson Plans of Phonics Wonder

Lesson Plan

Letters & Sounds
New target combinations of sounds and related words are introduced with pictures.

Read
Children practice reading words with the target sounds.

Write 1
Children practice identifying and writing the target double letters.

Write 2
Children confirm their understanding of the target words by writing them.

Listen
Children practice listening the target words.

Read Along!
Children further practice the target words reading simple story.

Listen & Write
Children practice listening and reading the target words in sentences.

Key Features

The Review provides practice of the materials from the previous two units by using a variety of exercises for the target sounds of letters and words.

The Final Review reinforces the material with a variety of exercises such as the reading of brief stories that include the sight words and playing games.

The Final Test consists of 20 listening comprehension questions and 14 reading questions that cover the target sounds of letters and words.

Introduction of the Multi-ROM

Main Menu

 **Sound**

Children practice the target sounds and the corresponding words.

 **Words**

Children listen and repeat the words with the target sounds.

 **Chant**

Children listen and repeat the target sounds and words in the chant.

 **Read Along**

Children read and repeat the key words with the target letters in the sentences.

 **Game**

Children play games using the target letters and words.

 **Check-Up**

Children take a brief test by listening and reading the target letters and words.

Details

 Children listen and repeat the target sounds and words by watching the shape of a native speaker's mouth.

 In **Words** corner, children write the target words by clicking their mouses.

 Children record their own pronunciation of the target words and check it by comparing it to the recording of a native speaker's pronunciation.

Unit 1 — ee ea

Listen and repeat. **Track 1**

e e → b e e

Track 2

 bee 

 tree 

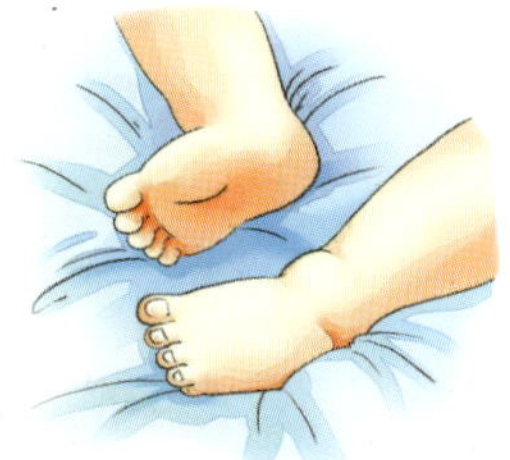 feet

 seed 

 peel

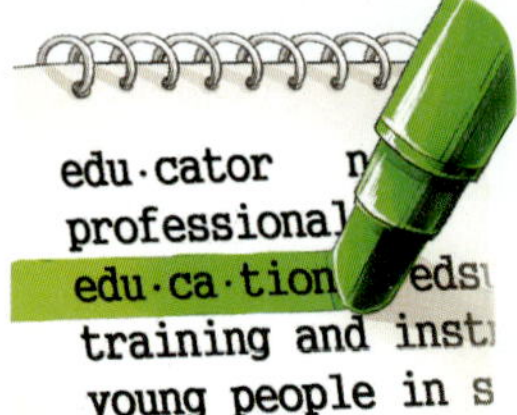 green 

Listen and repeat. 

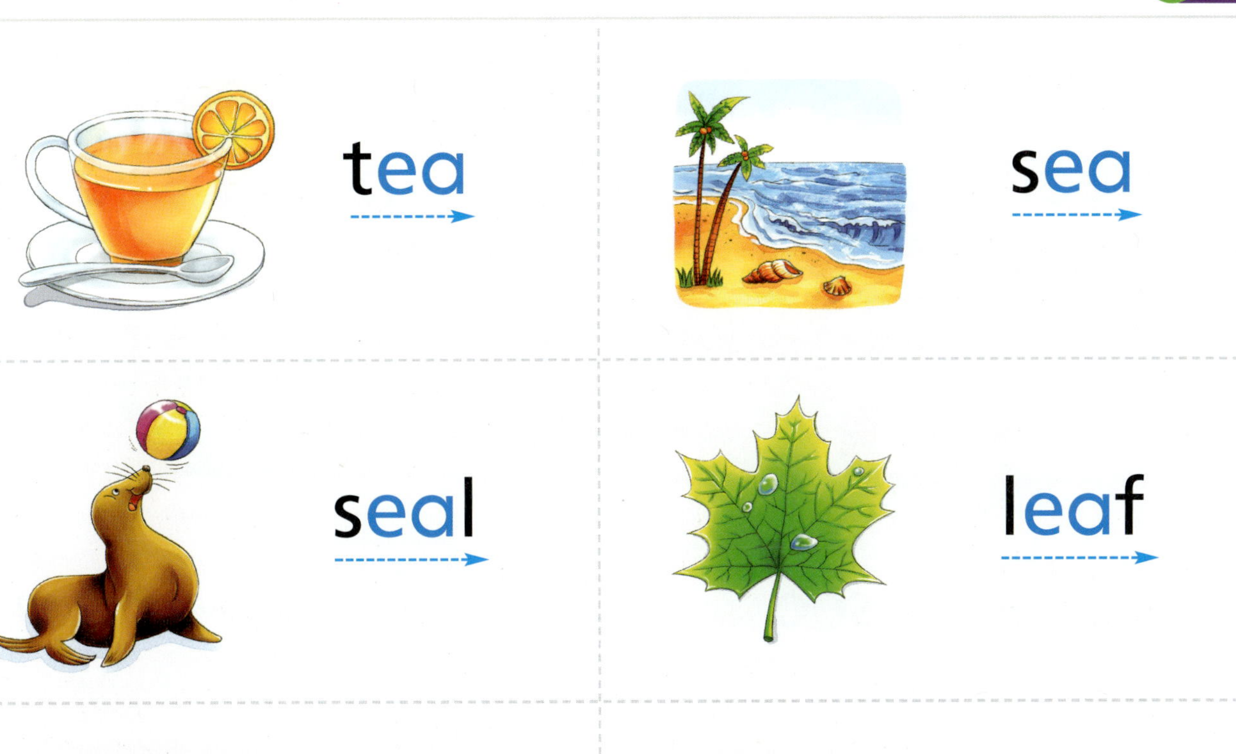

 **Let's chant!** 

Circle the correct word.

1 

sea   bee

2 

leaf   tree

3 

green   peanut

4 

peel   seal

5 

seed   sea

6 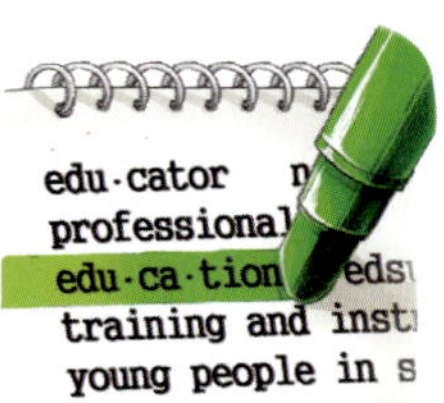

green   meat

7 

leaf   peel

8 

seal   tree

Write the correct letters.

1

s ___d

ee ea

2

b___

ee ea

3

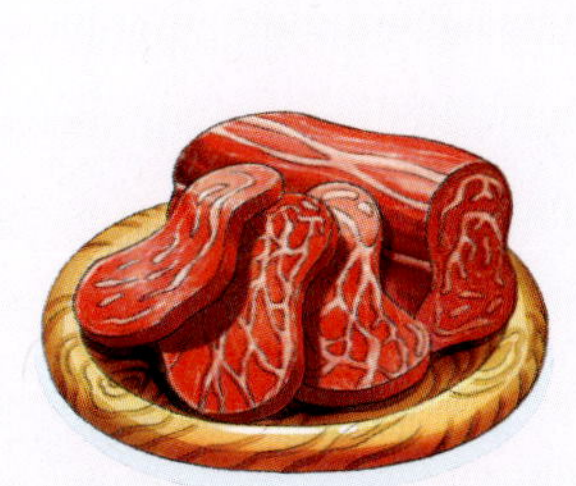

m___t

ee ea

4

l__f

ee ea

5

t___

ee ea

6

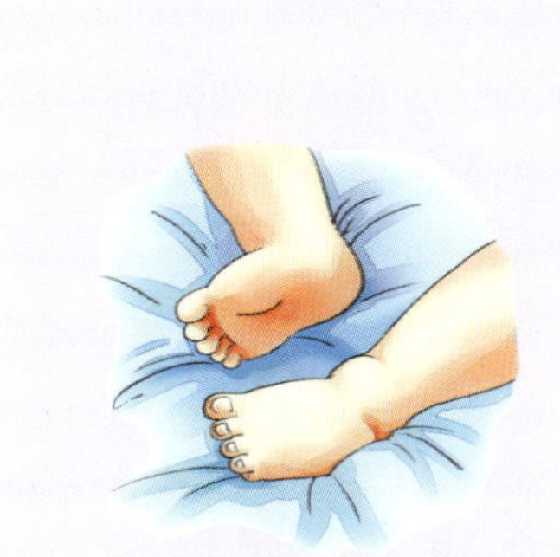

f___t

ee ea

Write the word in the correct column.

Listen and circle the correct picture. **Track 6**

Listen and check the correct word. **Track 7**

1	☐ peel	☐ tea	☐ seed	☐ feed
2	☐ bee	☐ seal	☐ leaf	☐ sea
3	☐ meat	☐ green	☐ peanut	☐ bee
4	☐ tree	☐ sea	☐ feet	☐ peel

Read Along!

A bee in a green tree says,

"I have six feet.

I don't like seeds and peel.

I like sweet flowers."

A seal in a blue sea says,

"I have four feet.

I don't like meat and peanuts.

I like fresh fish."

Listen and write the correct word. 

1 

The children are drinking ____________.

| tea | bee | tree |

2 

My house is near the ____________.

| seed | sea | bee |

3 

There is a ____________ on the rock.

| seal | leaf | meat |

4 

The Christmas ____________ is in the corner.

| tree | tea | seed |

5 

There is a banana ____________ on the ground.

| seal | peel | sea |

Unit 2 · ai ay

Listen and repeat.  **Track 10**

a i → r a i n

 **Track 11**

 rain

 mail

 train

 nail

 rail

 tail

Listen and repeat.  Track 12

a y → g gray

Track 13

gr**ay** →	cl**ay** →	
h**ay** →	pl**ay** →	
tr**ay** →	May →	

 Let's chant!  Track 14

Circle the correct word.

1 

nail   clay

2 

gray   train

3 

mail   play

4 

tray   snail

5 

tail   May

6 

rain   hay

7 

nail   gray

8 

play   tail

Write the correct letters.

1

tr＿＿n

ai　ay

2

pl＿＿

ai　ay

3

t＿＿l

ai　ay

4

gr＿＿

ai　ay

5

r＿＿n

ai　ay

6

h＿＿

ai　ay

Write the word in the correct column.

Listen and circle the correct picture. Track 15

Listen and check the correct word. Track 16

1	☐ gray	☐ train	☐ clay
2	☐ mail	☐ tray	☐ May
3	☐ nail	☐ play	☐ rain
4	☐ hay	☐ tail	☐ gray

A day in May,

what does Kevin do?

He drives a nail into the rail.

Hurry up! Hurry up!

The train is coming.

A day in May,

what does Sarah do?

She makes hay outside.

Hurry up! Hurry up!

It's going to rain.

Listen and write the correct word.  Track 18

1 

The ______________ comes at 7:10.

| train | hay | tray |

2 

She is wearing a ______________ coat.

| nail | gray | May |

3 

The monkey has a long ______________.

| tail | mail | clay |

4 

There are some fruits on the ______________.

| play | May | tray |

5 

The boy makes a house with ______________.

| snail | rain | clay |

Fill in the blanks and match the picture to the word.

Listen and circle the correct picture. Then complete the word. Track 19

1 __ e a __

2 __ a i __

3 __ __ a y

4 __ __ e e __

5 __ e e __

6 __ __ a y

7 __ __ a i __

8 __ e a

Listen and circle the correct word. Then match the picture.

1 feet / leaf

2 train / tail

3 hay / May

4 gray / green

5 tray / tree

6 seed / seal

7 rain / rail

8 play / clay

9 mail / meat

10 tea / bee

Listen to the sentences and circle the correct word. Then write the words in the puzzle. **Track 21**

↓ 1 Keep your (feet / seed) clean and dry.

➡ 2 The boy doesn't like (hay / peanut) butter.

➡ 3 The pig has a short (tail / leaf).

↓ 4 We have to leave for the (May / train).

↓ 5 The children (play / rail) in the playground.

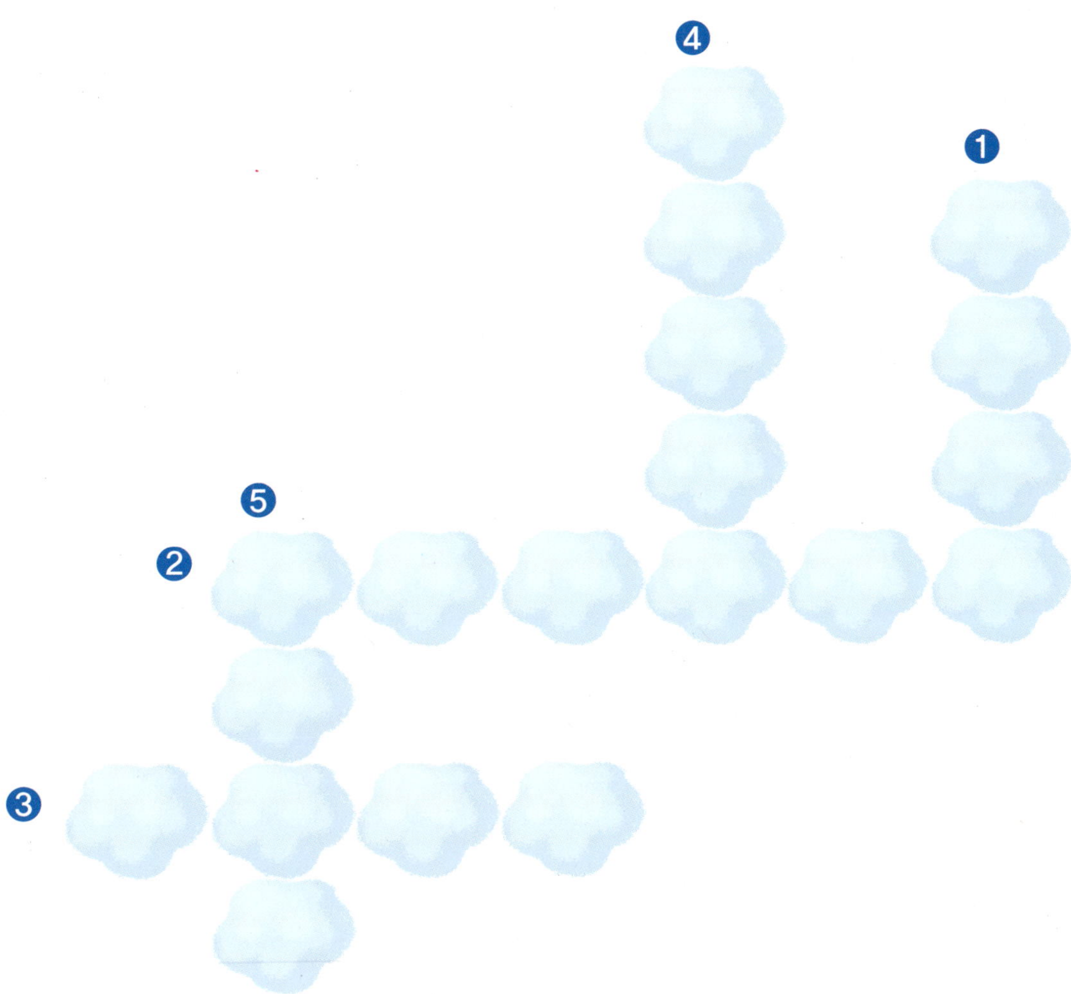

oa ow

Listen and repeat.  Track 22

o a → c o a t

 Track 23

coat

boat

soap

road

goat

toast

Listen and repeat. Track 24

Track 25

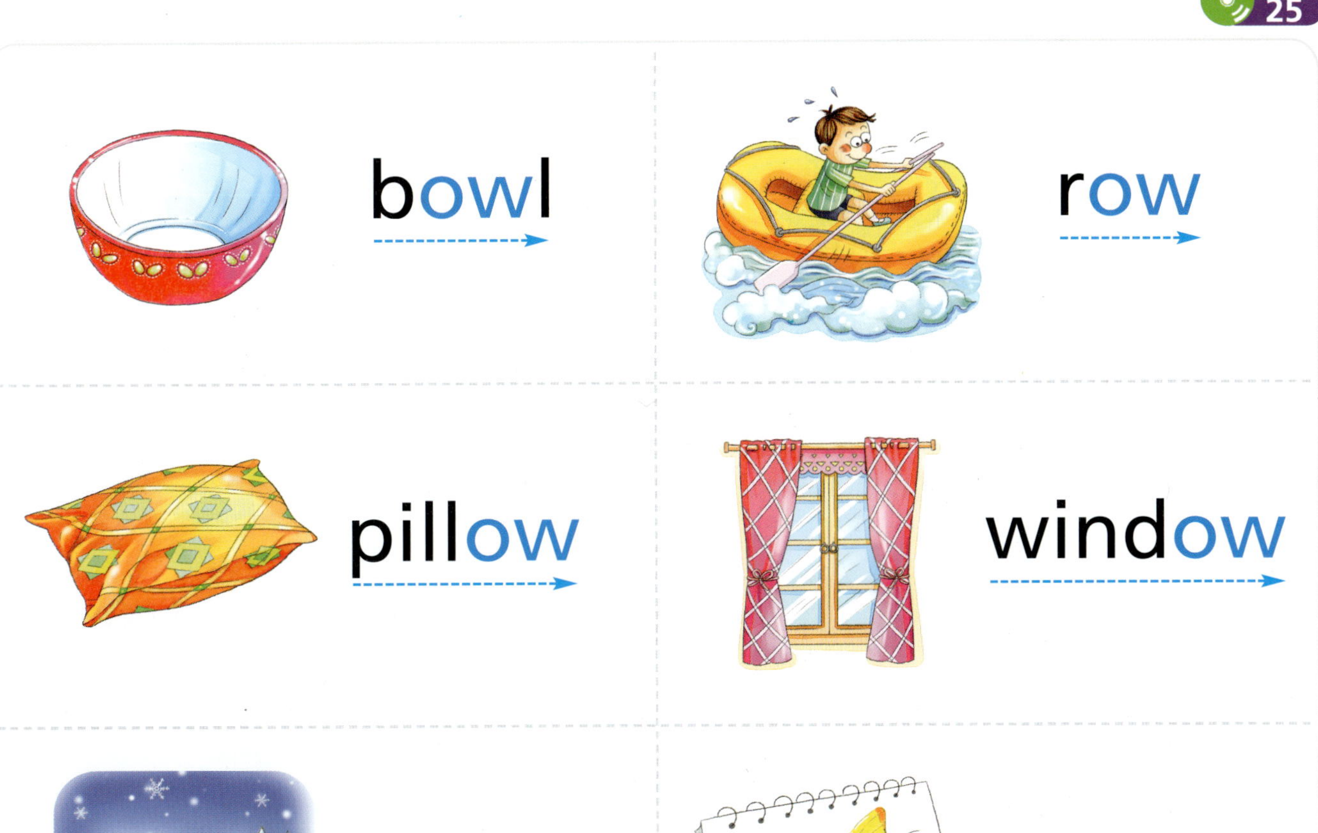

  **Let's chant!** Track 26

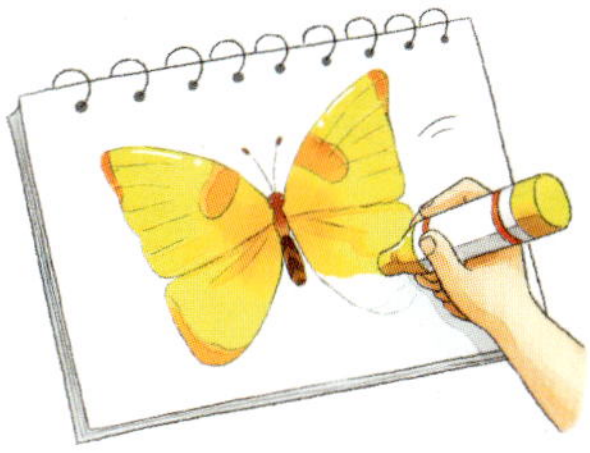

Circle the correct word.

1

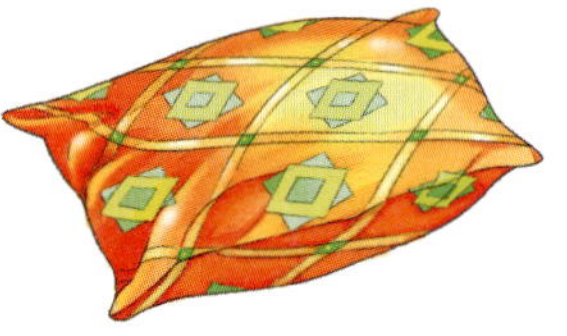

boat   pillow

2

soap   window

3

snow   toast

4

yellow   coat

5

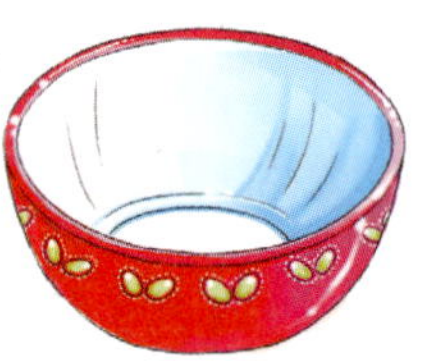

road   bowl

6

goat   row

7

coat   window

8

snow   road

Write the correct letters.

1

c___t   r___   oa ow

2

b___l   b___t   oa ow

3

r___d   wind___   oa ow

Write the word in the correct column.

Listen and circle the correct picture. **Track 27**

1   **2**

3   **4**

5   **6**

Listen and check the correct word. **Track 28**

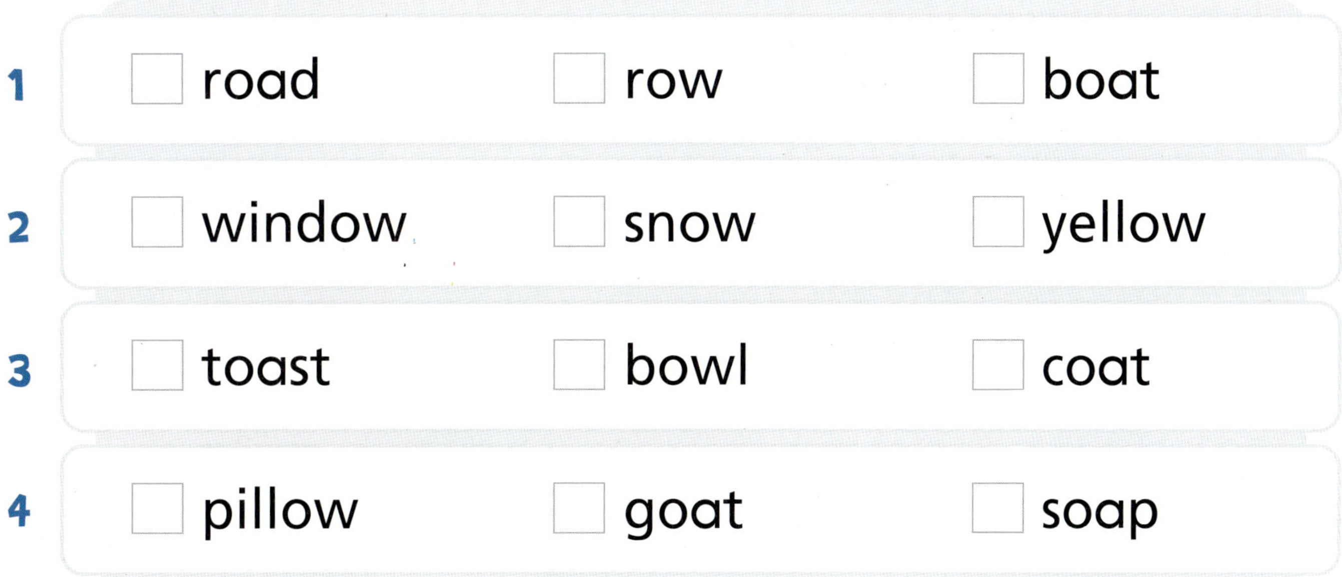

1	☐ road	☐ row	☐ boat
2	☐ window	☐ snow	☐ yellow
3	☐ toast	☐ bowl	☐ coat
4	☐ pillow	☐ goat	☐ soap

Read Along!

There's a goat on the road.

Oh! It looks dirty.

Let's give it a bath.

Use the soap! Wash off the dirt!

There is toast in the bowl.

Oh! It smells delicious.

Let's eat it together.

Everyone, it's snack time!

Listen and write the correct word. 

1 

A _____________ is floating on the water.

2 

The child is wearing a _____________ sweater.

3 

The _____________ falls fast.

4 

A brown _____________ is on the bed.

5 

The man eats _____________ for lunch.

oi oy

Listen and repeat.  Track 31

 Track 32

 coin 

 boil 

 soil 

 oil 

 foil 

 coil 

 Track 33

Track 34

toy

boy

oyster

joy

soybean

royal

Let's chant!

Track 35

Circle the correct word.

1 

oil   boy

2 

oyster   soil

3 

foil   joy

4 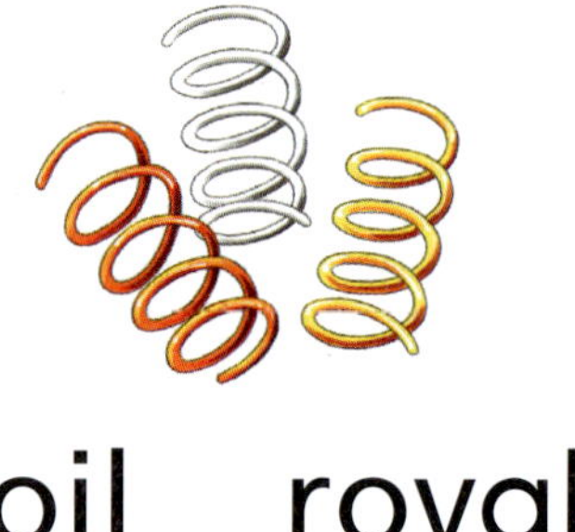

coil   royal

5 

boil   toy

6 

boy   coin

7 

soybean   oil

8 

toy   foil

Write the correct letters.

1

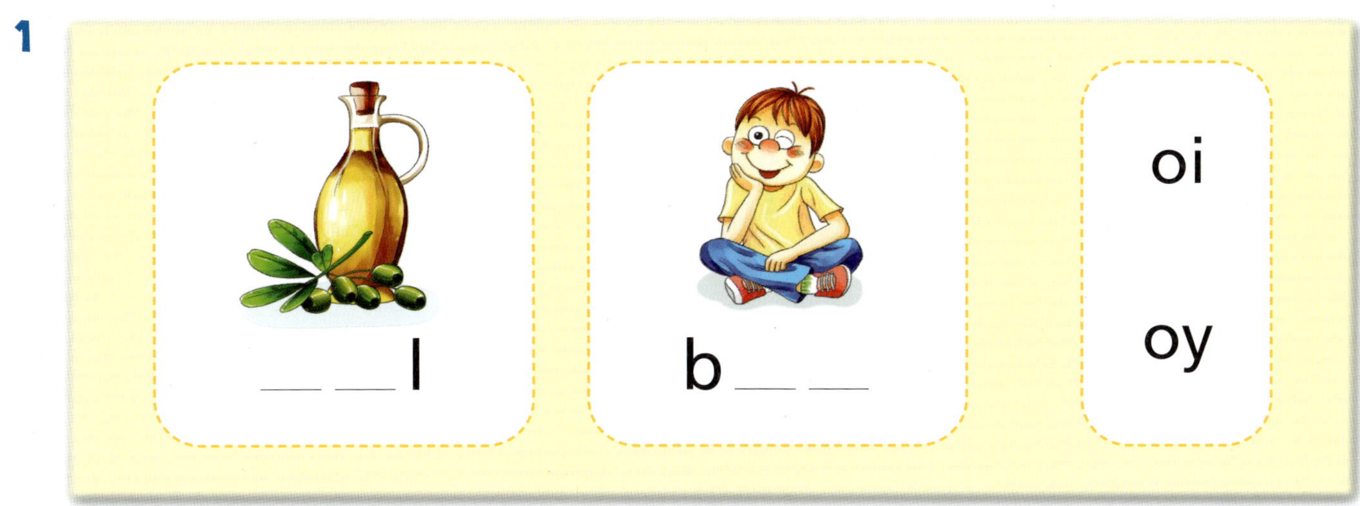

2

3

Write the word in the correct column.

Listen and circle the correct picture. Track 36

Listen and check the correct word. Track 37

1	☐ toy	☐ coin	☐ oil
2	☐ joy	☐ soybean	☐ royal
3	☐ foil	☐ boy	☐ boil
4	☐ soil	☐ coil	☐ oyster

Read Along!

I am a boy cook, David.
I'll make a delicious dish.
I put some soybeans and water in the pot.
Now I boil it on the stove.
Wow! It smells good.

I am a girl cook, Dana.
I'll make a delicious dish.
I wrap some oysters and oil in foil.
Then I cook it on the grill.
Wow! It tastes great.

Listen and write the correct word. **Track 39**

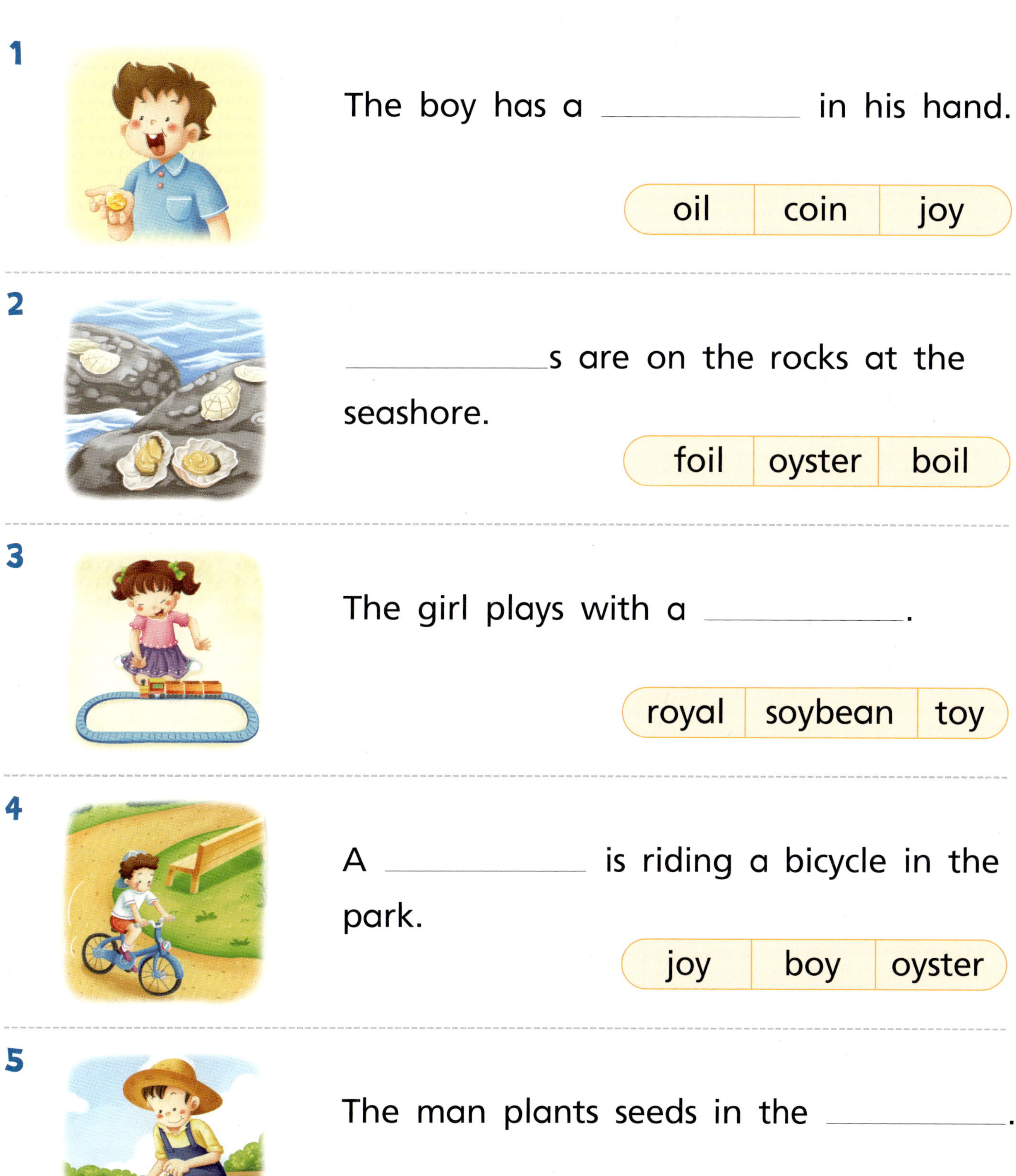

1

The boy has a _____________ in his hand.

| oil | coin | joy |

2

_____________s are on the rocks at the seashore.

| foil | oyster | boil |

3

The girl plays with a _____________.

| royal | soybean | toy |

4

A _____________ is riding a bicycle in the park.

| joy | boy | oyster |

5

The man plants seeds in the _____________.

| soil | royal | coil |

Review 2

Fill in the blanks and match the picture to the word.

oa   oy   ow   oi

1

2

3

4

- r＿＿al
- s＿＿l
- pill＿＿＿
- r＿＿d
- c＿＿t
- b＿＿l
- ＿＿ster
- c＿＿n

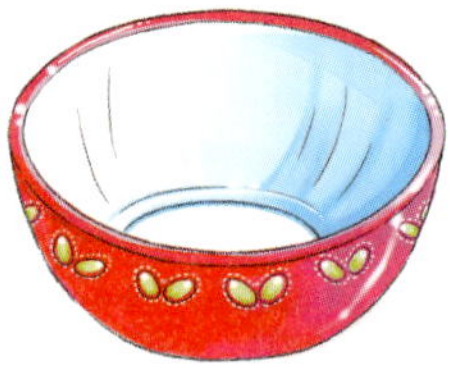

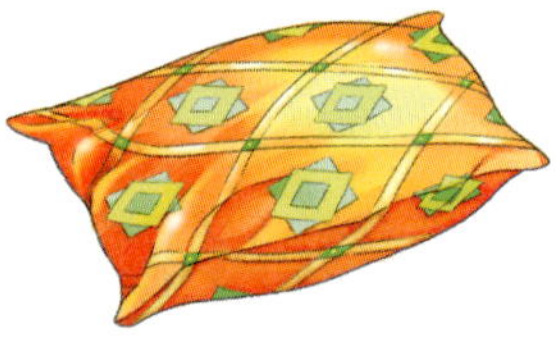

5

6

7

8

Listen and circle the correct picture. Then complete the word. Track 40

1 ___ ___ ow

2 ___ oi ___

3 ___ oa ___ ___

4 ___ oy

5 ___ oa ___

6 ___ oy ___ ___ ___ ___

7 ___ ow ___

8 ___ oi ___

Listen and circle the correct word. Then match the picture.

1
window
pillow

2
boat
toast

3
soil
soybean

4
road
goat

5
coat
coil

6
boil
foil

7
snow
row

8
joy
toy

9
oil
boy

10
soap
soil

Listen to the word and circle the correct balloon.  Track 42

1 soap window

2 coin boat

3 goat foil

4 pillow royal

5 soil joy

6 toy row

7 road boat

8 oyster bowl

OU OW

Listen and repeat.  Track 43

| o | u | → | m | o | u | s | e |

 Track 44

mouse

cloud

house

south

ground

blouse

Listen and repeat. **Track 45**

Track 46

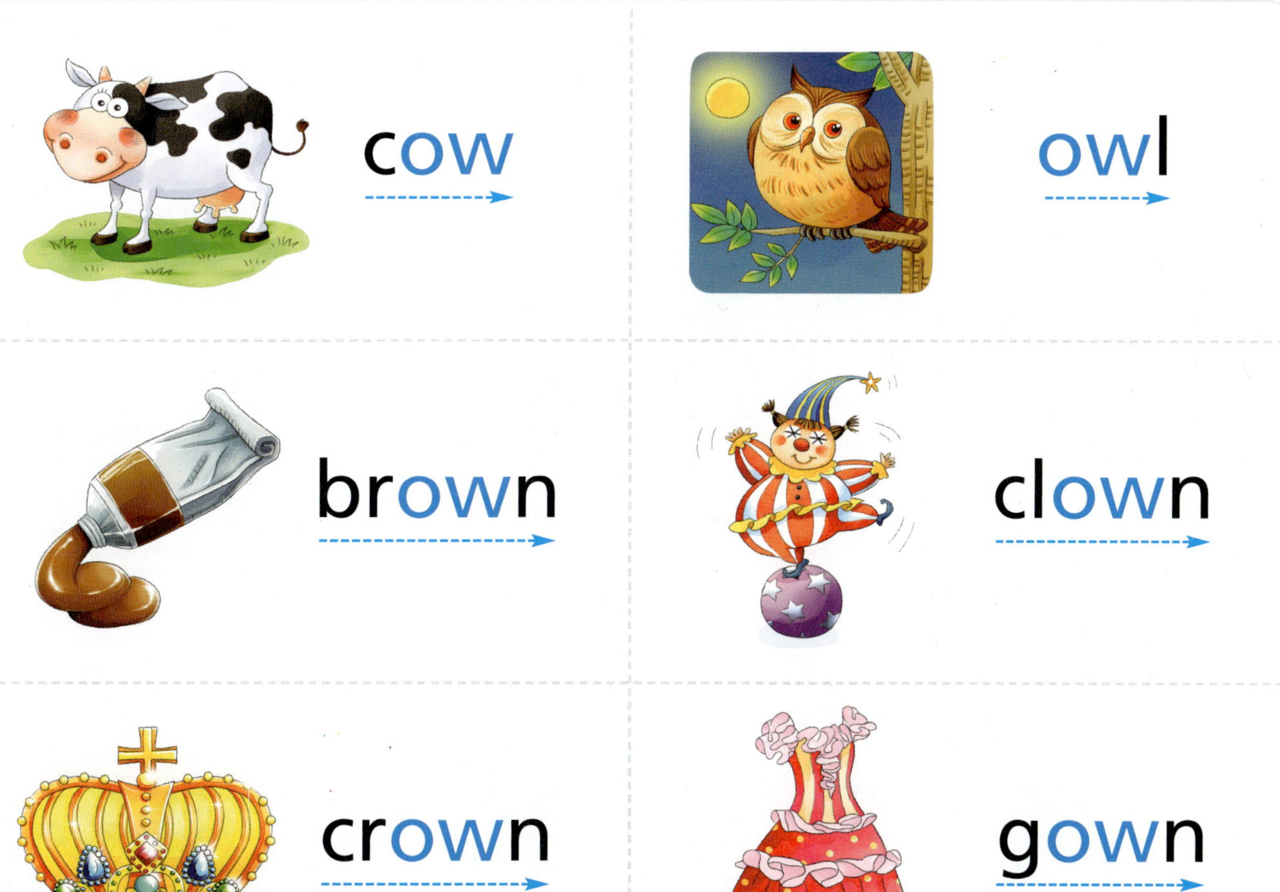

Let's chant!  **Track 47**

Write the correct letters.

ou   ow

1 gr__ __nd

2 c__ __ __

3 g__ __n

4 bl__ __se

5 __ __l

6 cl__ __d

7 s__ __th

8 m__ __se

9 br__ __n

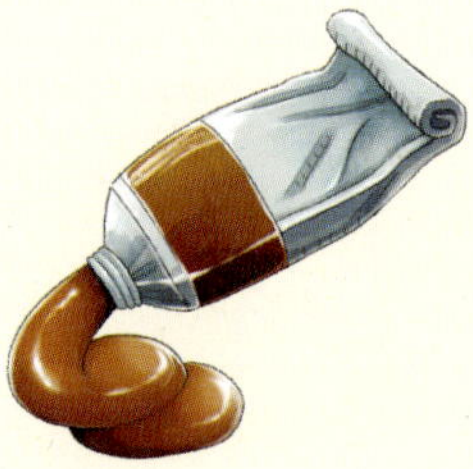

Circle and write the word for the picture.

1

2

3

4

5

6

Fill in the missing letters and write the word in the correct column.

Listen, then circle the correct picture and double letters.

Listen and write the correct word.

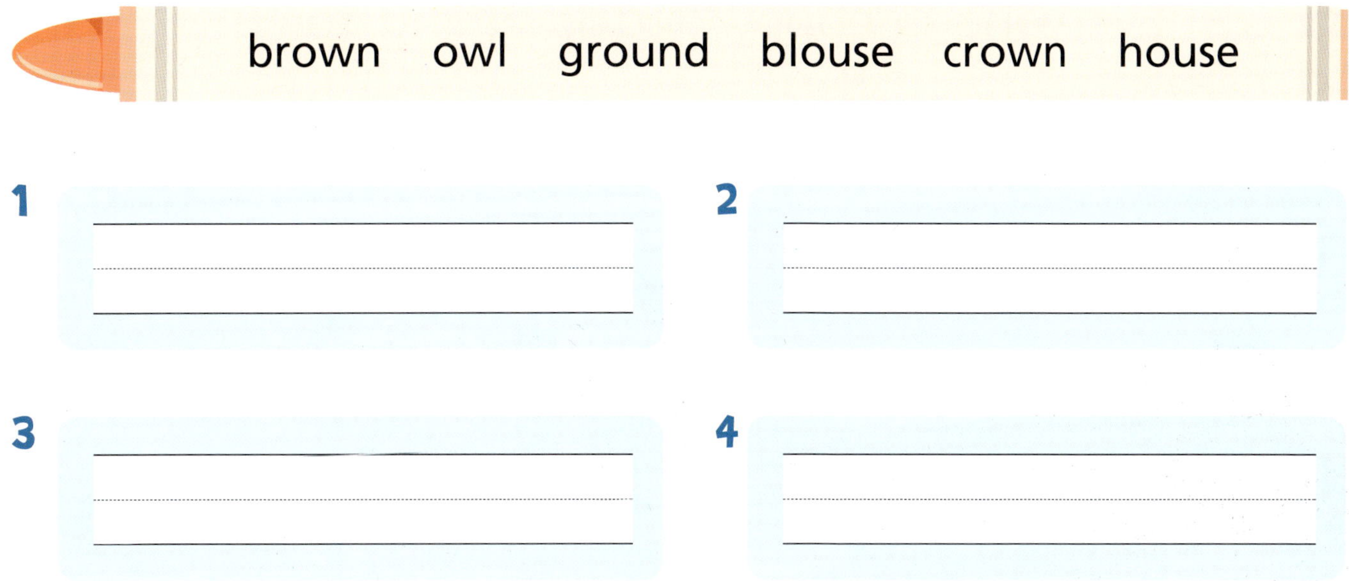

1

2

3

4

Read Along!

Track 50

It's a parade night.

Let's get nicely dressed.

Put on a red gown like a king.

Wear a gold crown like a queen.

An owl flies in the clouds.

A mouse dances on the ground.

A clown plays the violin in the crowd.

Everyone is happy and laughing tonight.

Listen and write the correct word. 

1

The _______________ gives a girl some flowers.

| clown | mouse | gown |

2

_______________s are eating grass in the field.

| mouth | owl | cow |

3

A woman is wearing a white wedding _______________.

| gown | blouse | cow |

4

The _______________ is on the branch.

| owl | crown | mouse |

5

The _______________ looks like a sheep.

| cloud | house | blouse |

Unit 6 — oo

Listen and repeat. Track 52

o o → m o o n

Track 53

moon	spoon
root	goose
pool	broom

Listen and repeat. Track 54

o o → b o o k

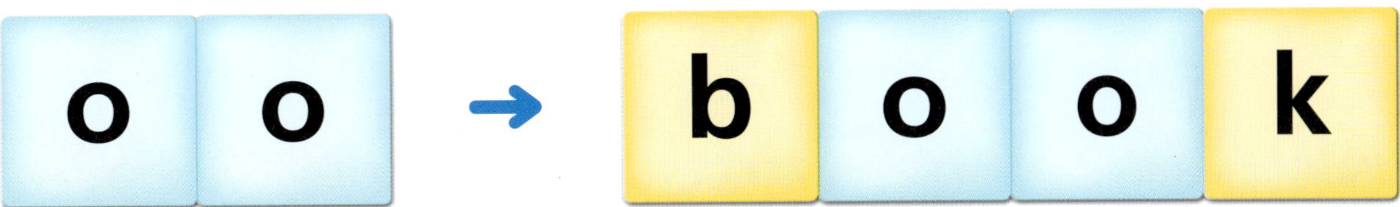

Track 55

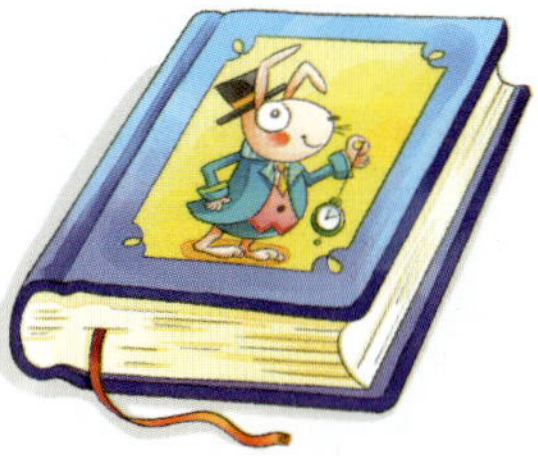

book

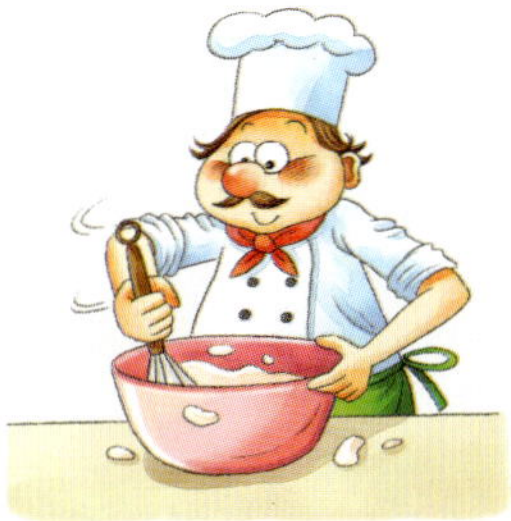

cook

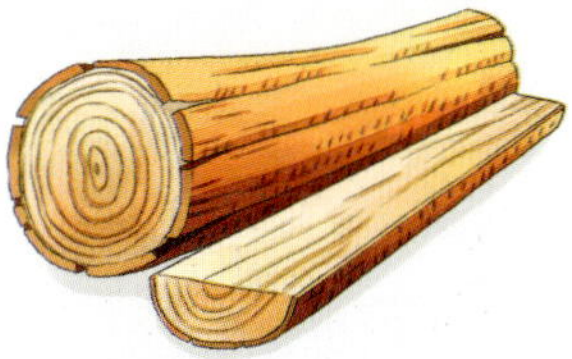

wood

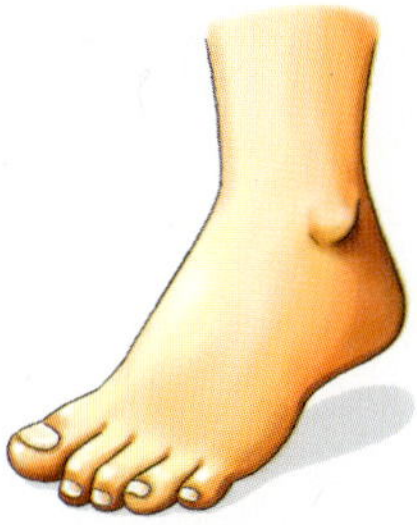

foot

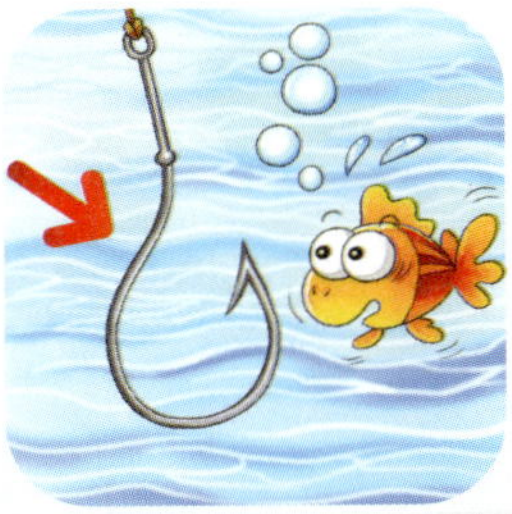

hook

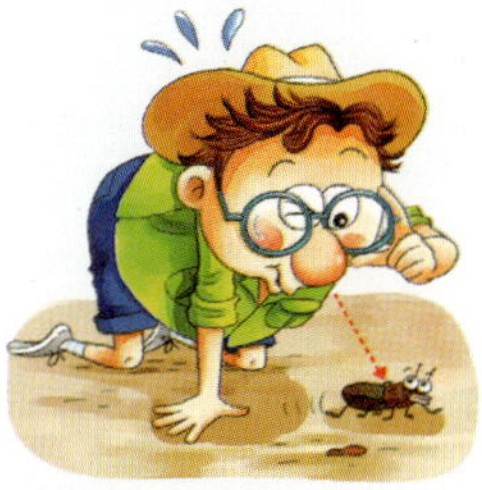

look

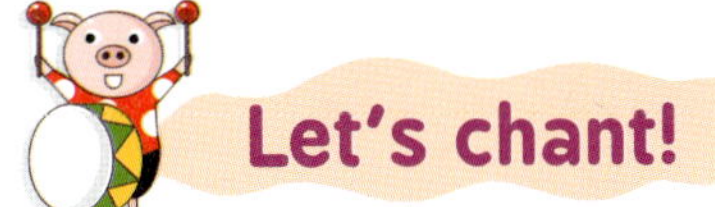

Let's chant! Track 56

Circle the picture with the same vowel sound as the first picture.

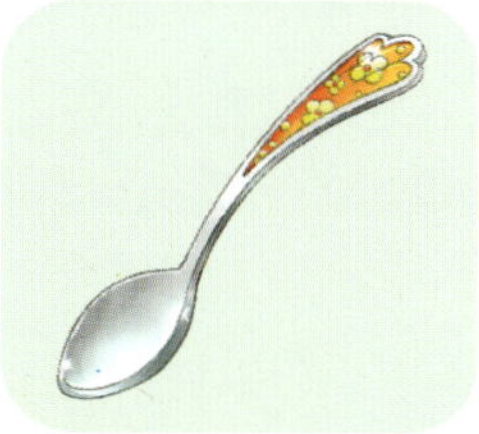

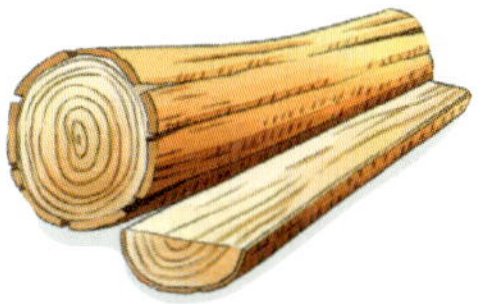

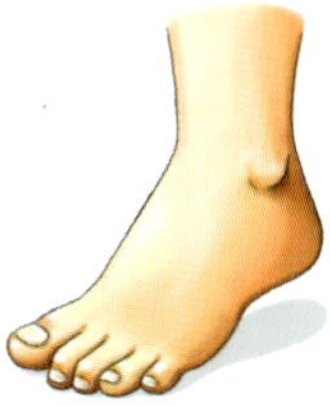

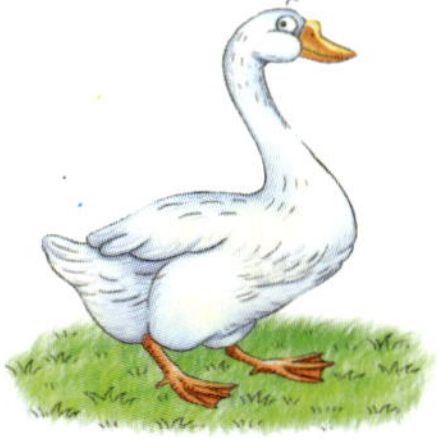

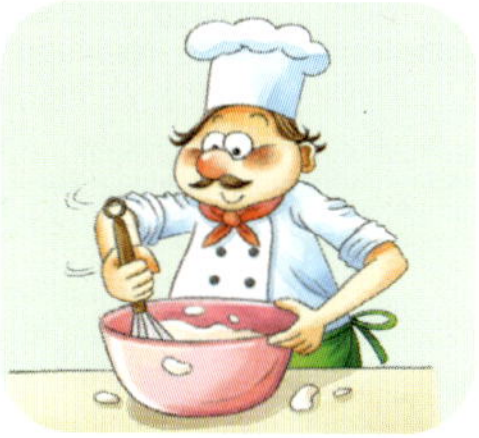

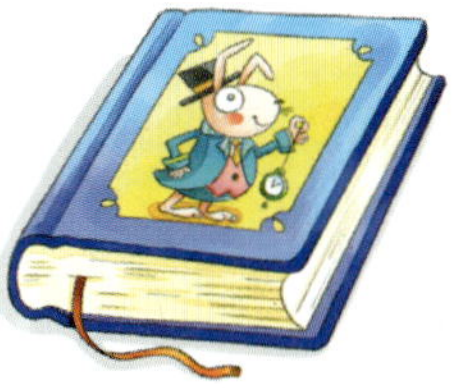

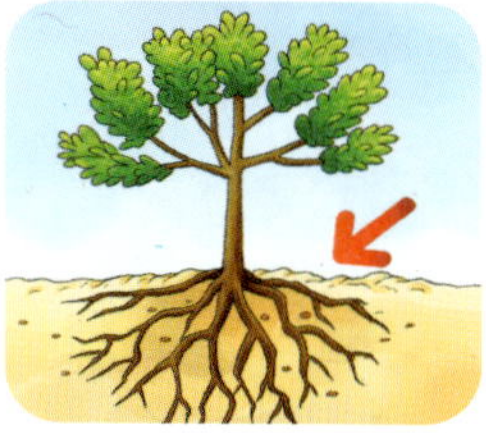

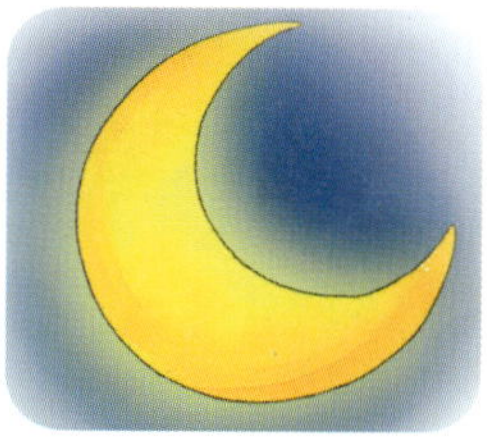

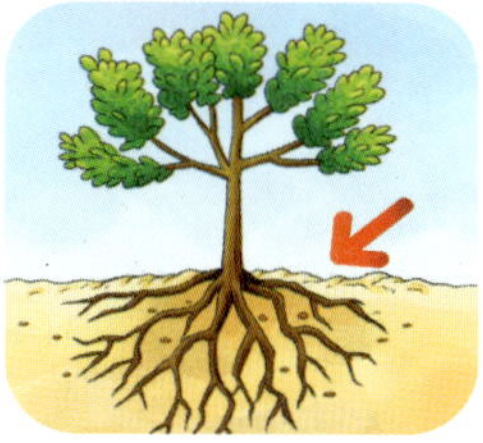

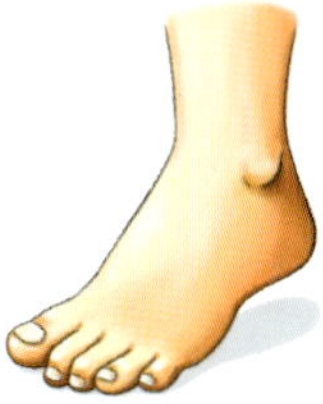

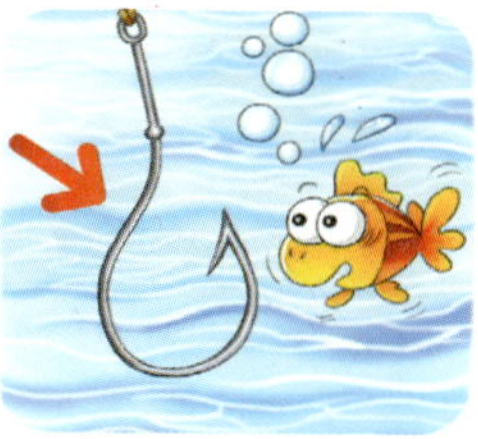

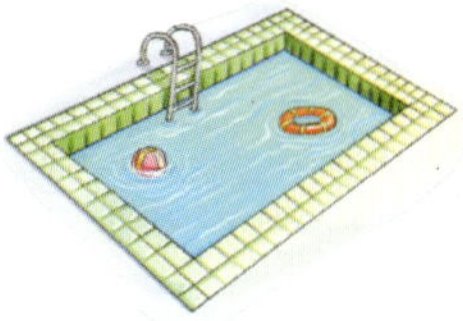

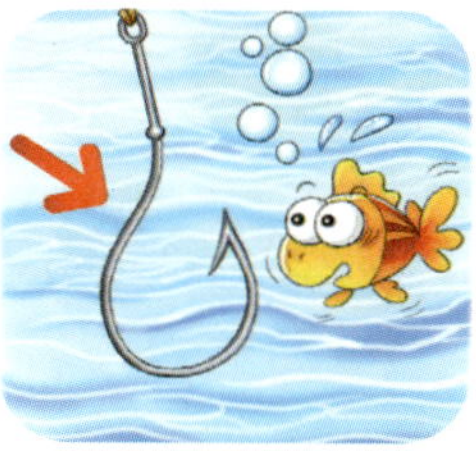

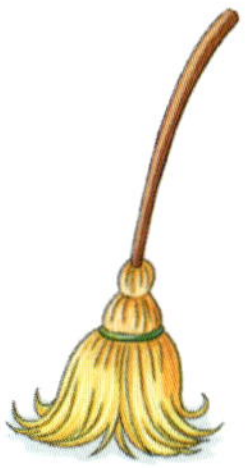

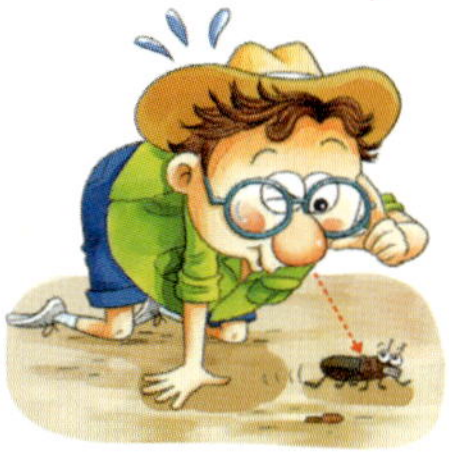

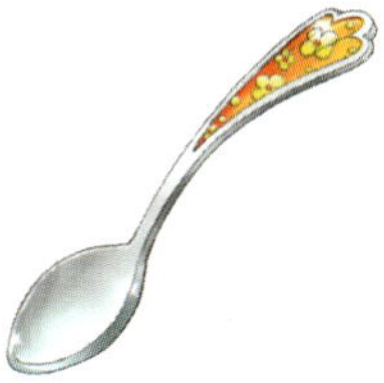

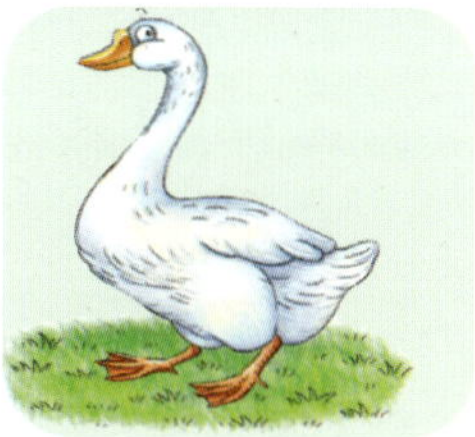

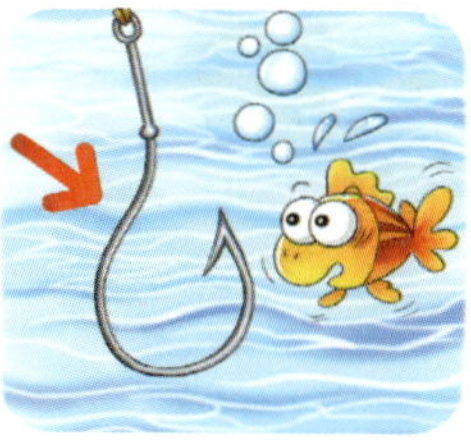

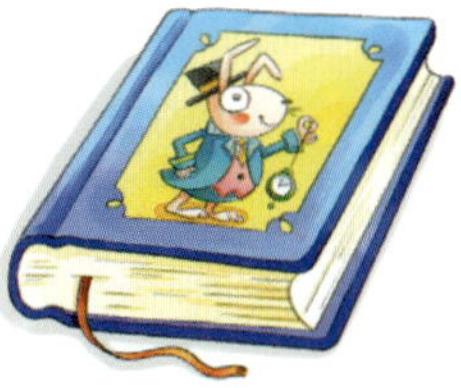

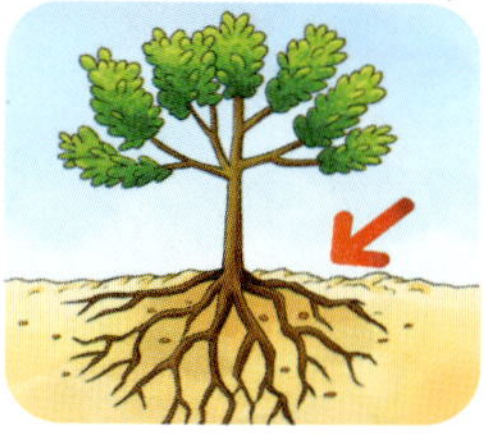

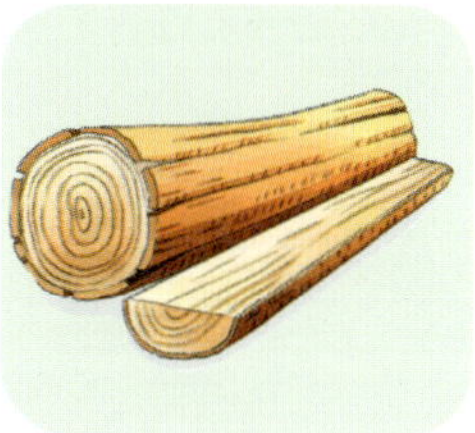

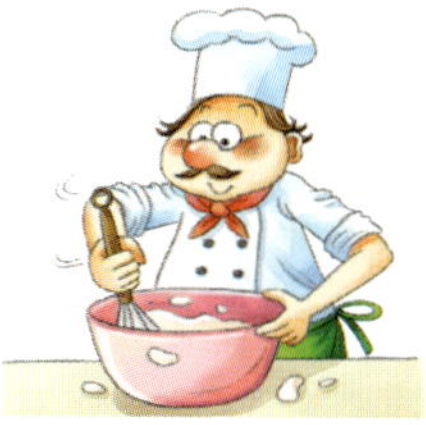

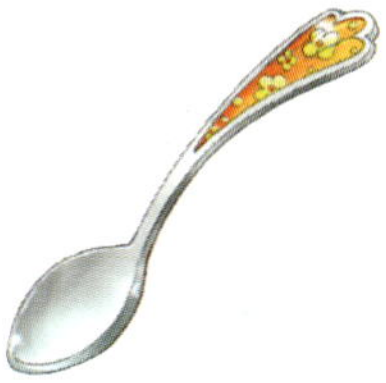

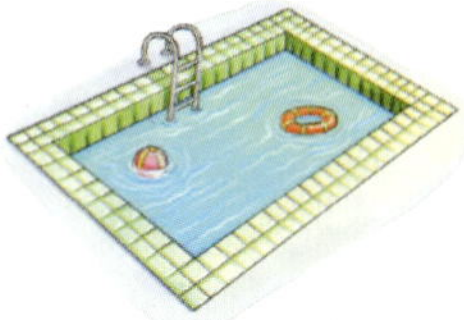

1

s t **c o o k** l t

2

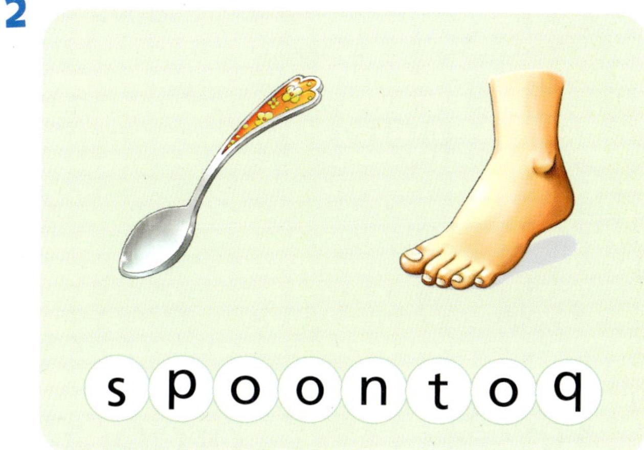

s p o o n t o q

3

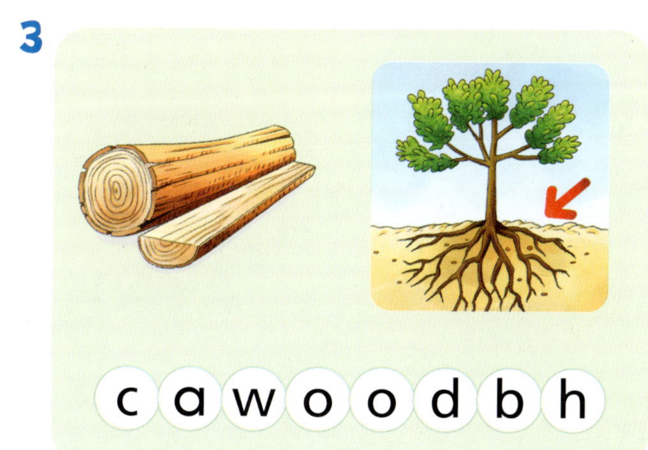

c a w o o d b h

4

i j e d p o o l

5

g o o s e h y r

6

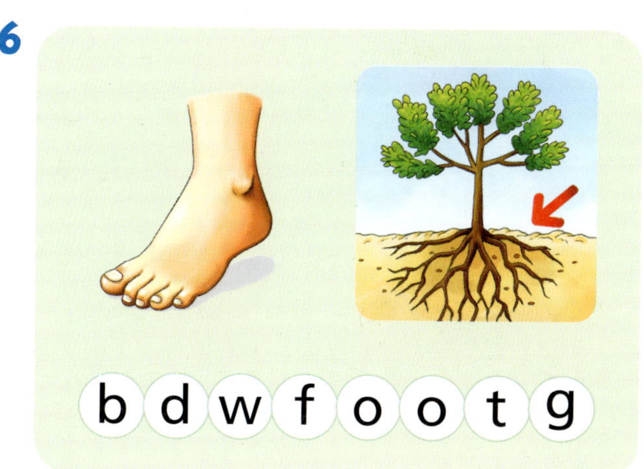

b d w f o o t g

Write the word in the correct column.

pool

wood

goose

hook

broom

look

foot

root

Listen, number and match the picture to the word. 

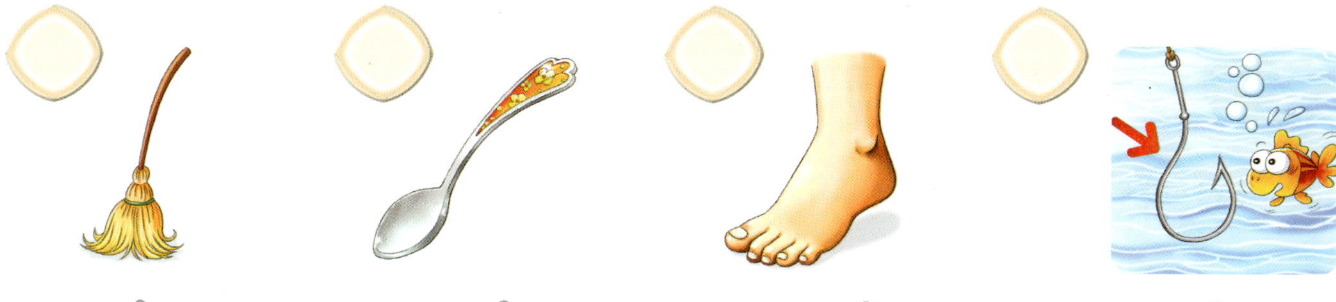

foot   broom   spoon   hook

Listen and write the correct word. 

root   broom   moon   book   look   foot

1

2

3

4

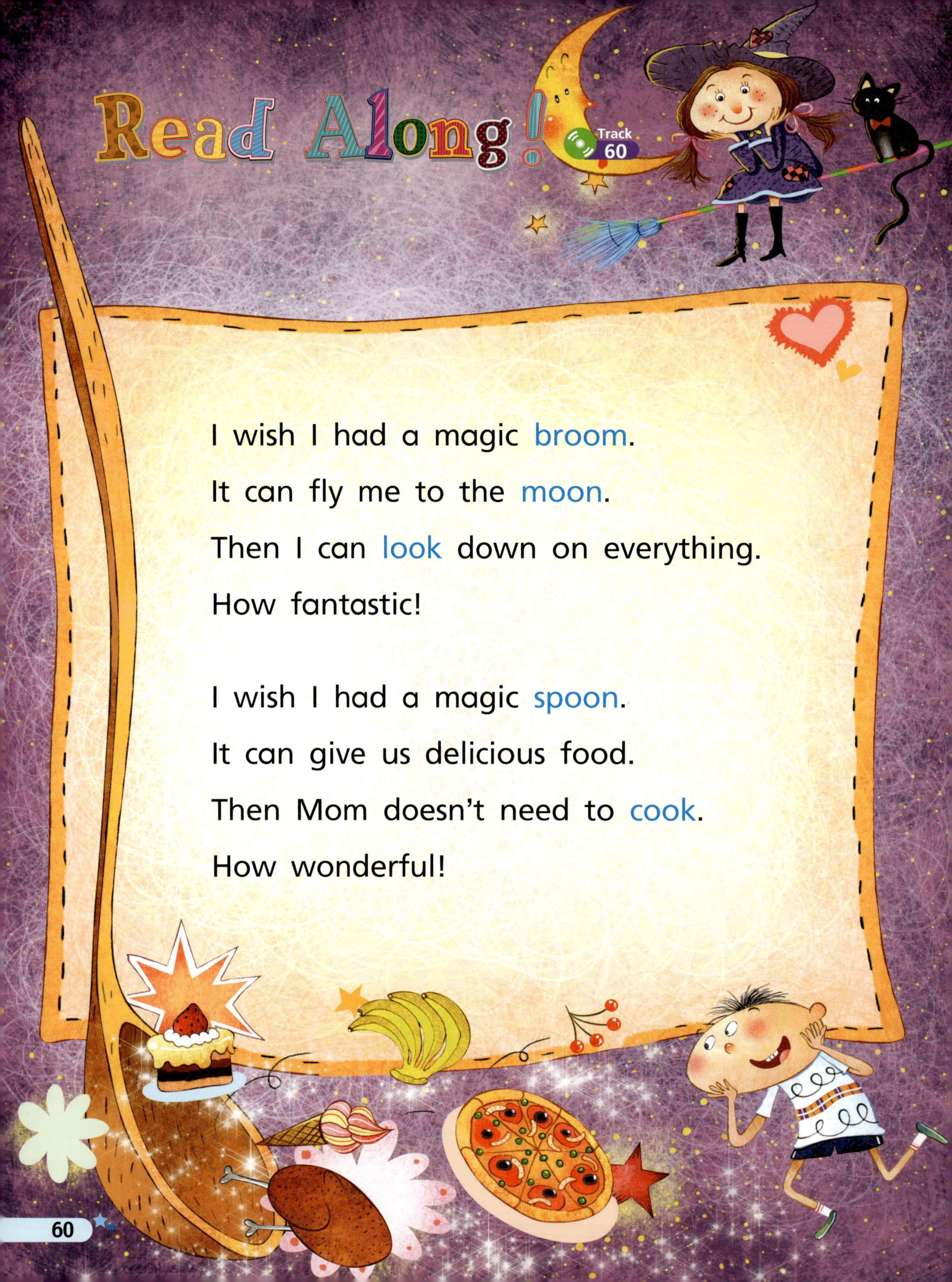

Read Along!

I wish I had a magic broom.

It can fly me to the moon.

Then I can look down on everything.

How fantastic!

I wish I had a magic spoon.

It can give us delicious food.

Then Mom doesn't need to cook.

How wonderful!

Listen and write the correct word. Track 61

1

The _____________ puts a pot on the stove.

| moon | cook | spoon |

2

The _____________ lays a golden egg.

| broom | goose | book |

3

A boy is reading a _____________ in the classroom.

| book | cook | foot |

4

There is a water slide in the _____________.

| wood | pool | moon |

5

The baby holds a _____________ to eat breakfast.

| hook | spoon | root |

Connect the letters to complete the word.

1

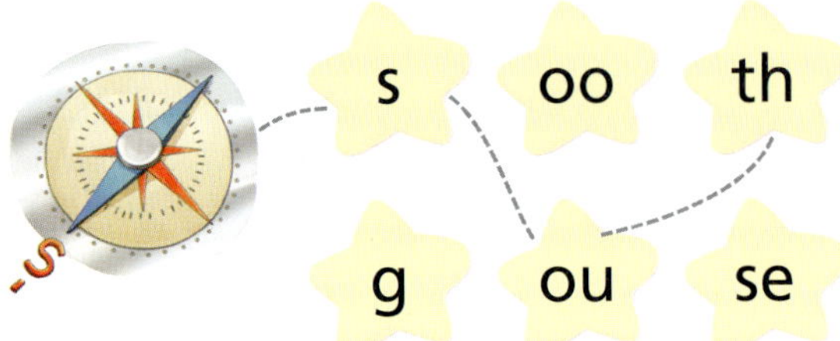

s	oo	th
g	ou	se

2

cr	ow	n
br	oo	m

3

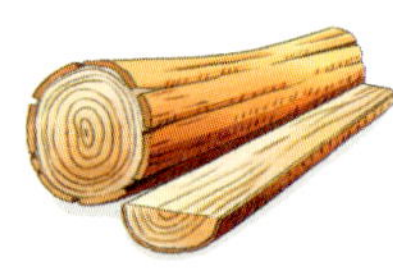

g	oo	d
w	ow	n

4

sp	ou	n
gr	oo	nd

5

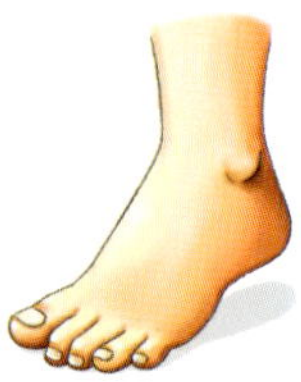

f	oo	t
r	ou	d

6

p	oo	n
h	ow	l

7

br	ow	th
m	ou	n

8

r	ou	t
g	oo	n

Listen and circle the correct picture. Then complete the word. **Track 62**

Listen and unscramble the letters. Then match the correct picture. **Track 63**

1 duorng → __________ •

• 

2 nowrc → __________ •

• 

3 moobr → __________ •

• 

4 kooh → __________ •

• 

5 lpoo → __________ •

• 

6 nwrbo → __________ •

• 

7 ookc → __________ •

• 

8 doulc → __________ •

• 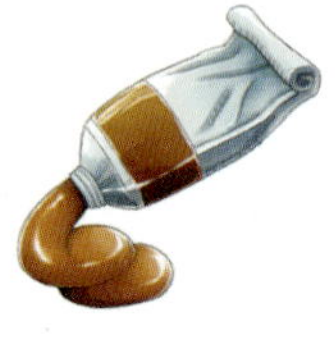

Listen to the sentence and fill in the missing word. Track 64

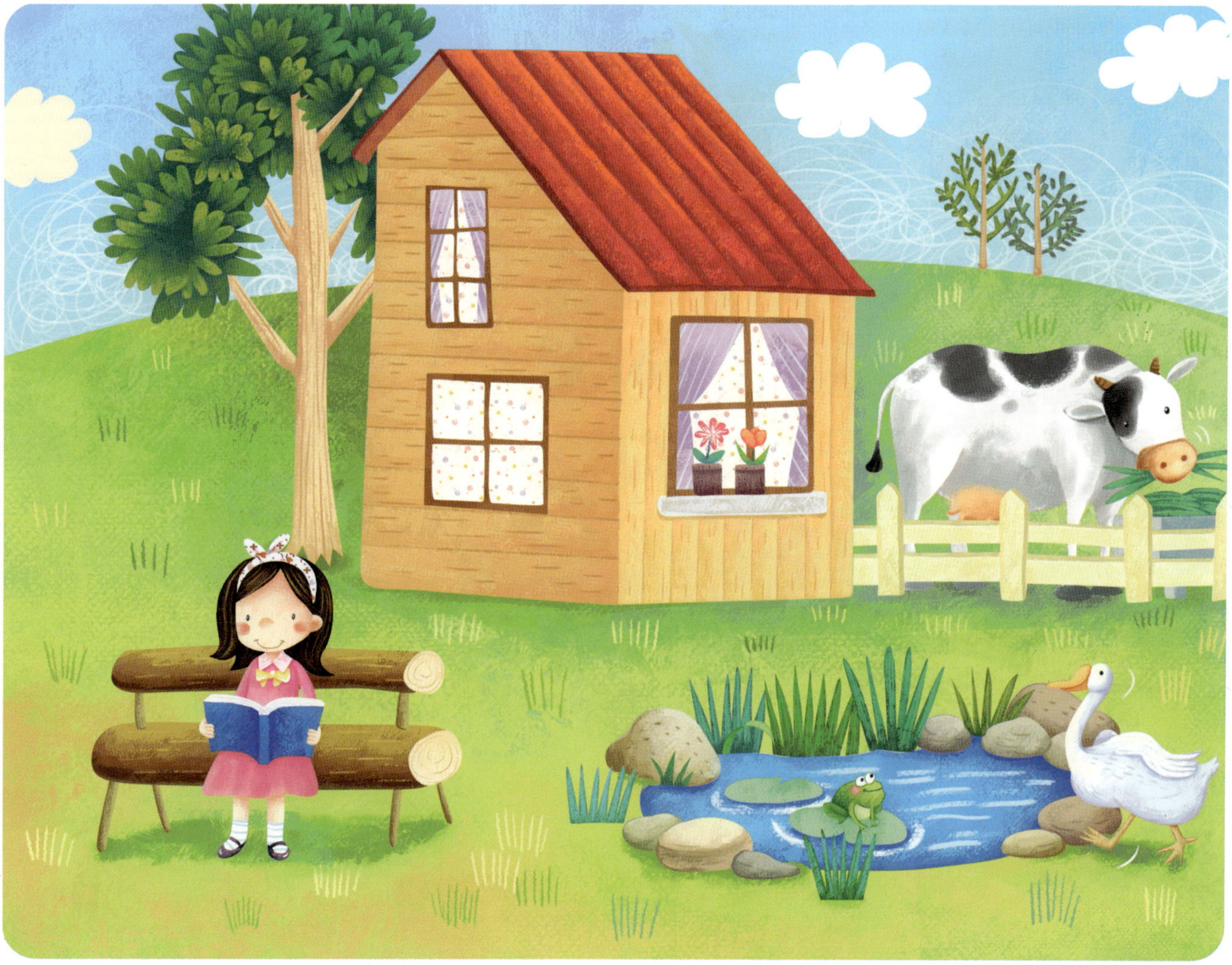

1 A girl is reading a ☐☐☐☐ on a bench.

2 The ☐☐☐ is eating some grass by the fence.

3 A ☐☐☐☐☐ has a red roof and big windows.

4 There is a ☐☐☐☐☐ next to the pond.

ar or

Listen and repeat. 

a **r** → **s** **t** **a** **r**

st**ar**

c**ar**d

f**ar**mer

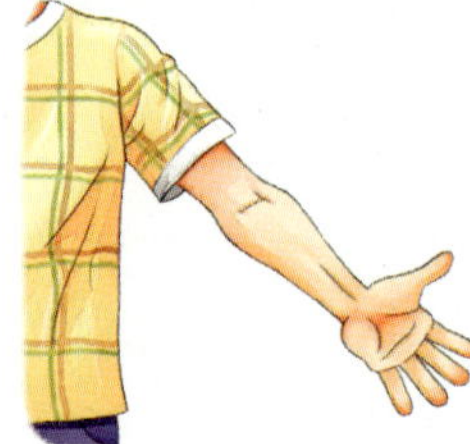

arm

p**ar**k

sh**ar**k

Listen and repeat. Track 67

o r → f o r k

Track 68

fork

horn

north

corn

horse

store

Let's chant! Track 69

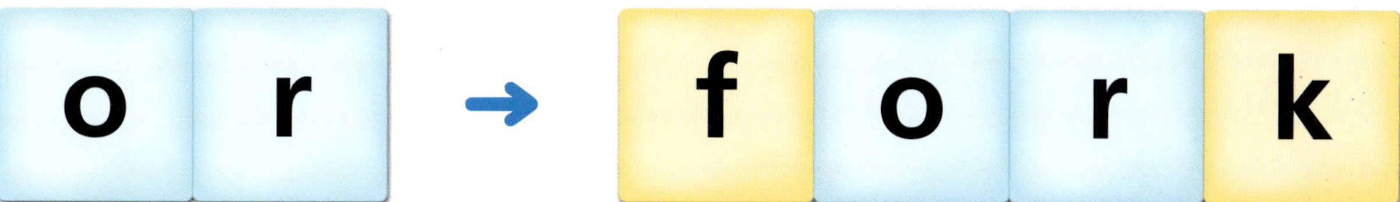

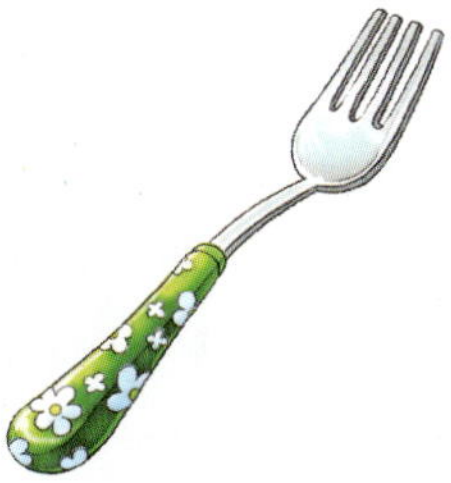

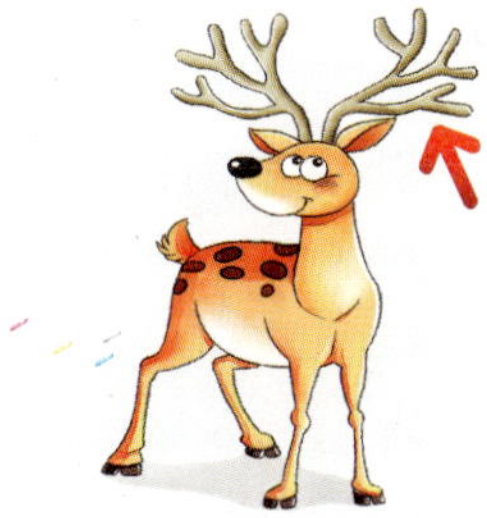

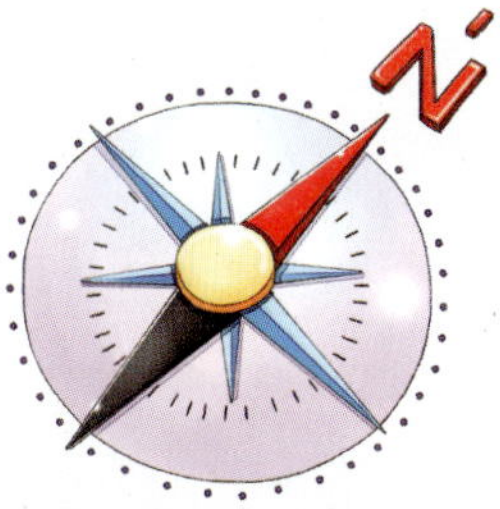

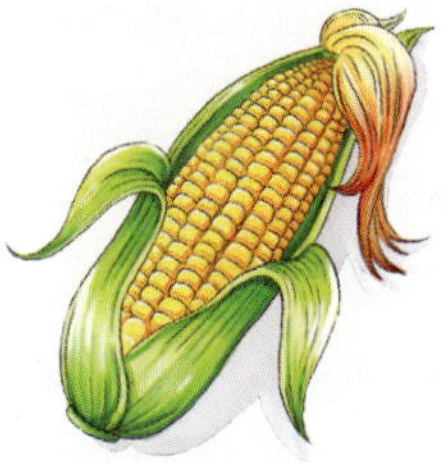

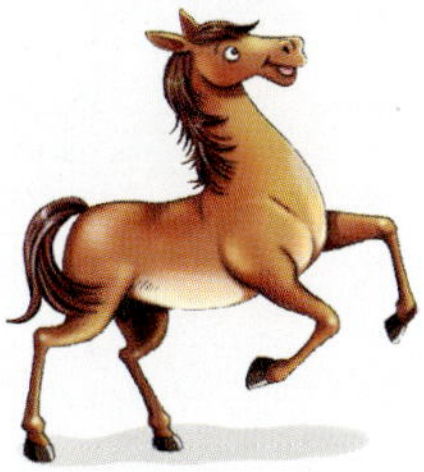

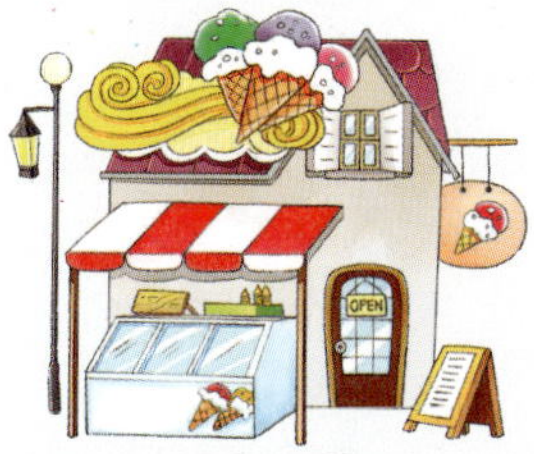

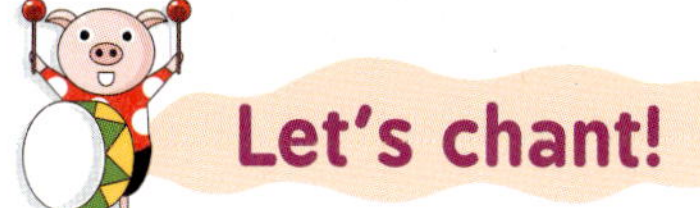

Check the pictures with the same vowel sound as the first picture.

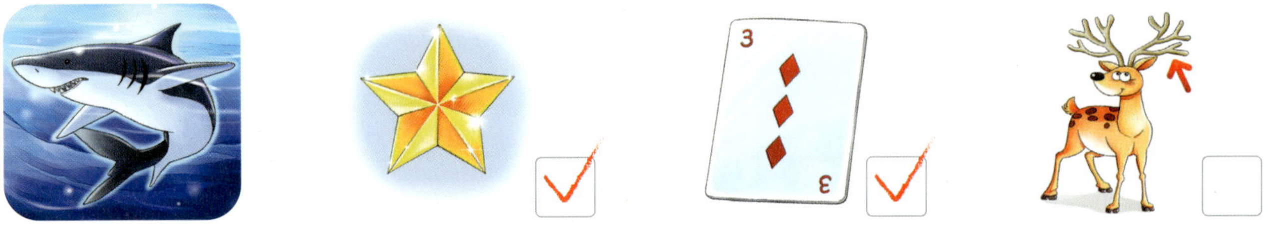

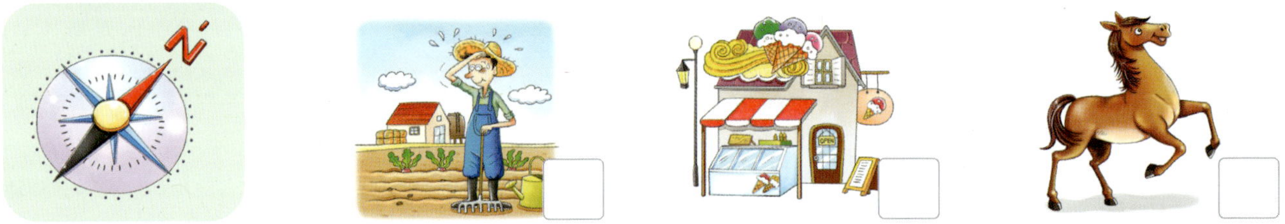

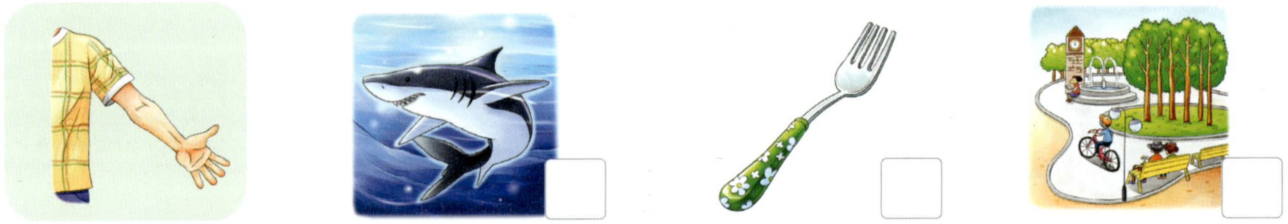

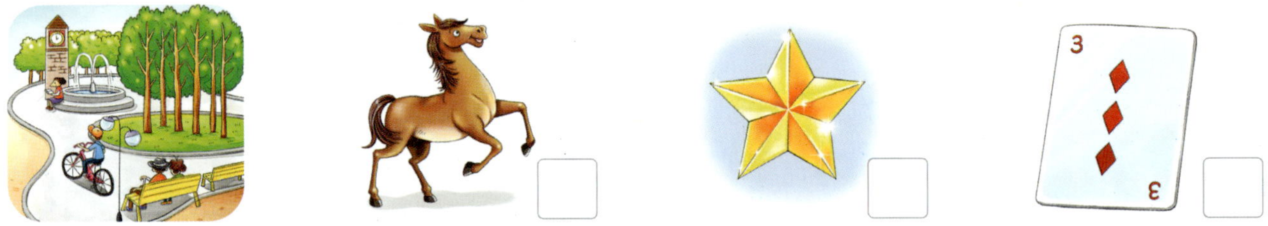

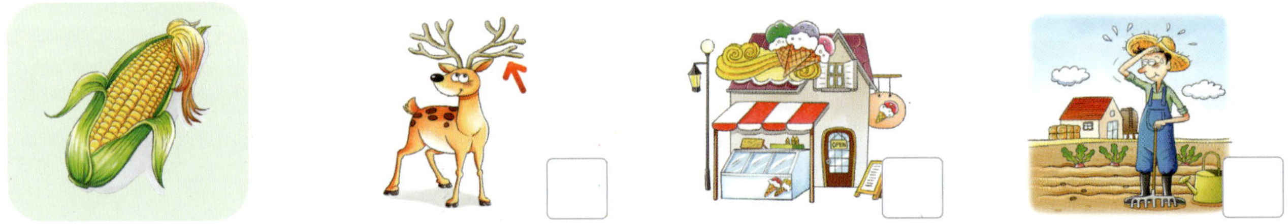

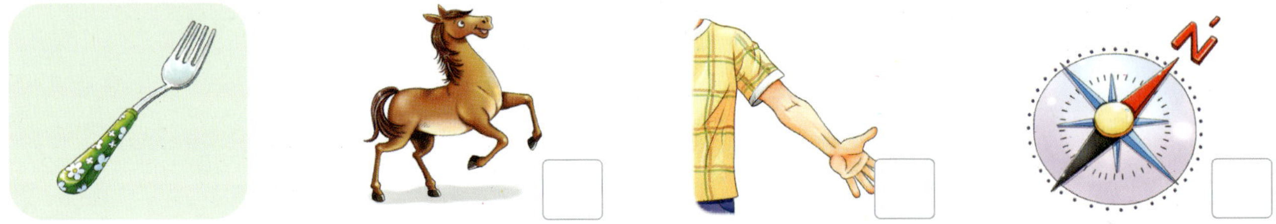

Circle and write the word for the picture.

1 

2 

3 

4 

5 

6 

Write the word in the correct column.

Listen, then circle the correct picture and double letters.

1   ar   or

2   ar   or

3   ar   or

4   ar   or

Listen and unscramble the letters. Then write the word.

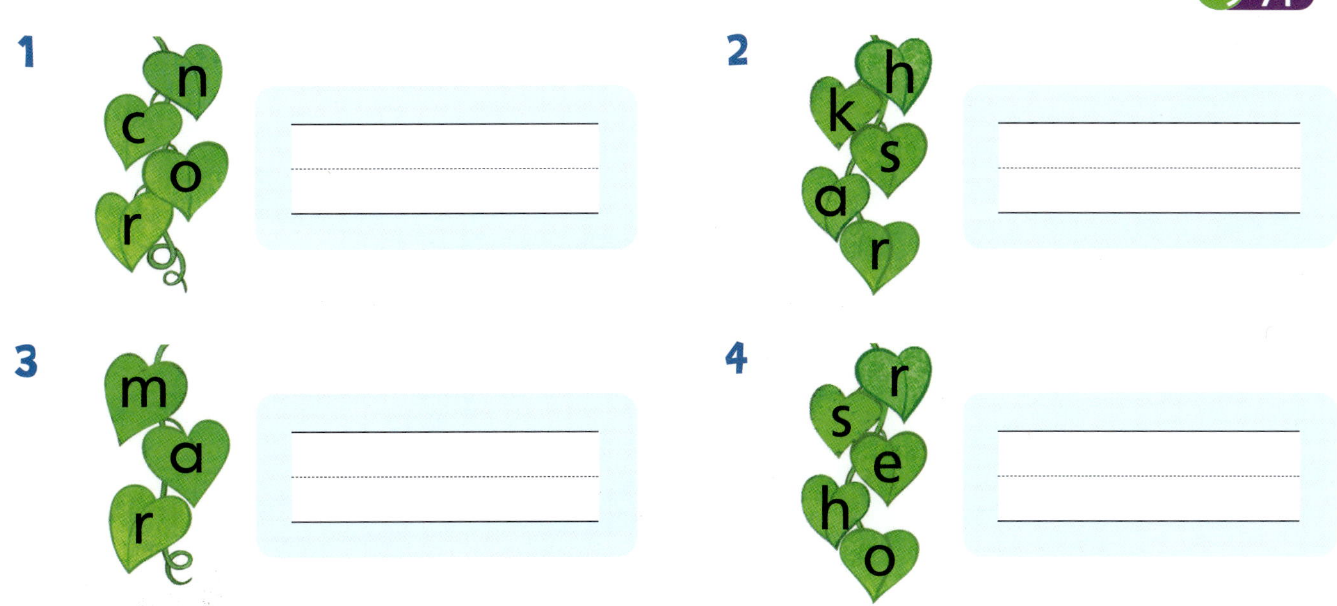

Read Along!

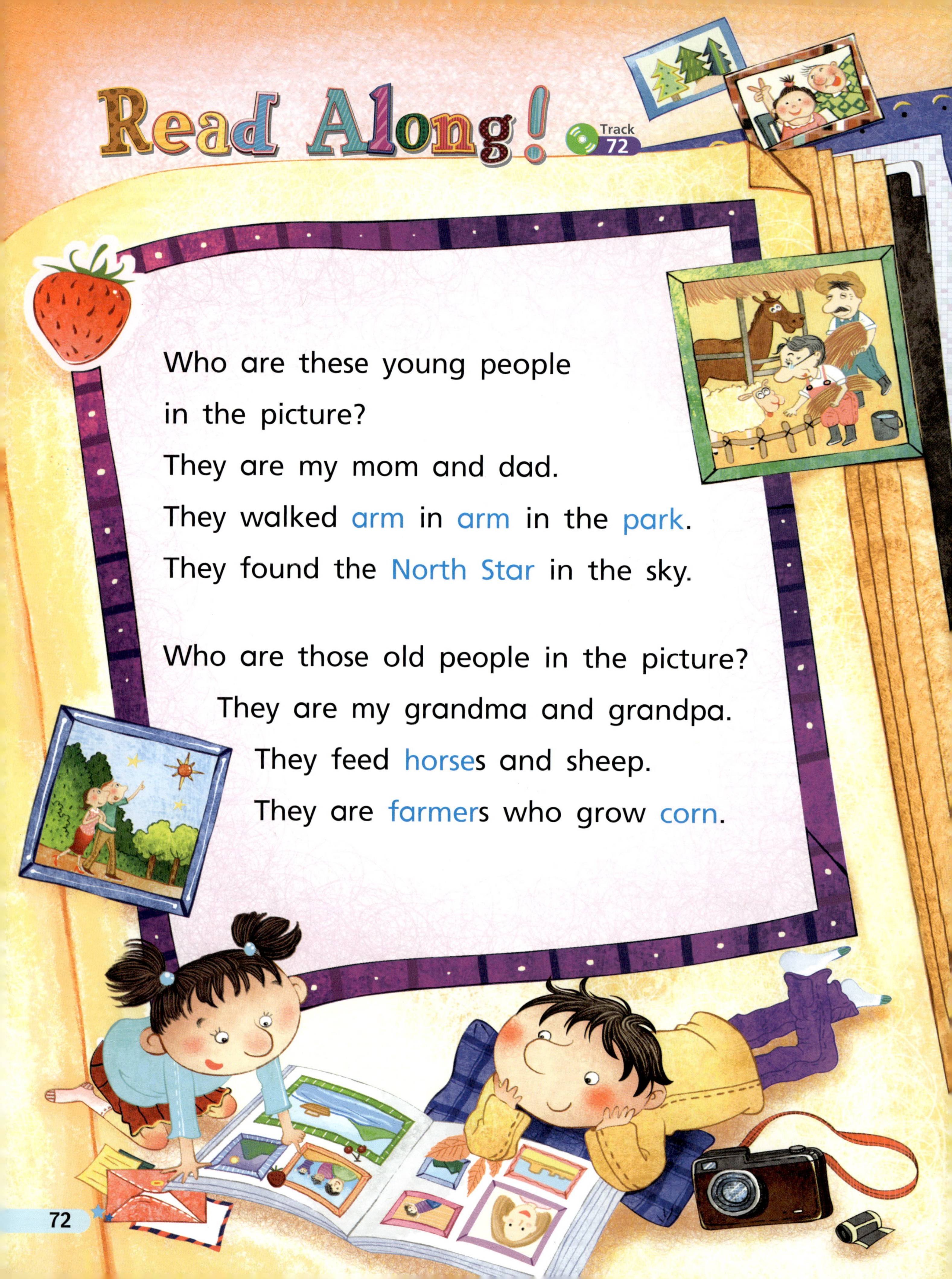

Who are these young people

in the picture?

They are my mom and dad.

They walked arm in arm in the park.

They found the North Star in the sky.

Who are those old people in the picture?

They are my grandma and grandpa.

They feed horses and sheep.

They are farmers who grow corn.

Listen and write the correct word. 

1 

There is a _____________ in the aquarium.

| corn | shark | fork |

2 

The spoon and _____________ are on the table.

| fork | card | horn |

3 

The children have _____________ for lunch.

| park | north | corn |

4 

A _____________ is shining brightly in the sky.

| horse | star | store |

5 

There are many people in the _____________.

| store | park | card |

er ur ir

Listen and repeat. 

er

flow**er**

lett**er**

socc**er**

ur

p**ur**se

n**ur**se

t**ur**tle

Listen and repeat. Track 76

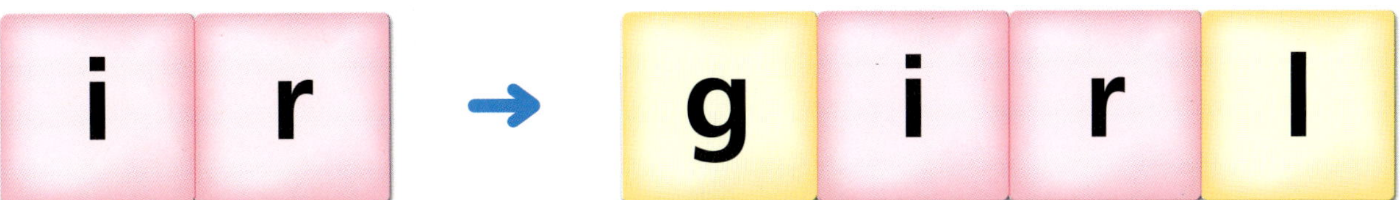

i r → g i r l

Track 77

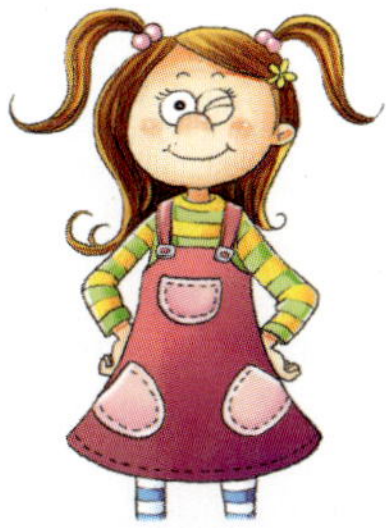

girl

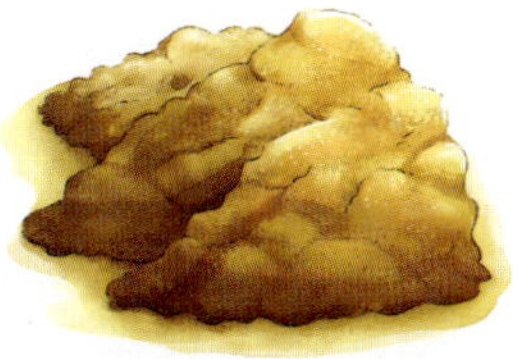

dirt

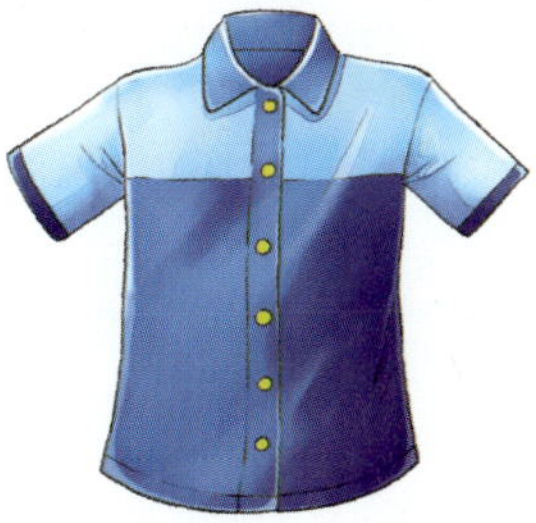

shirt

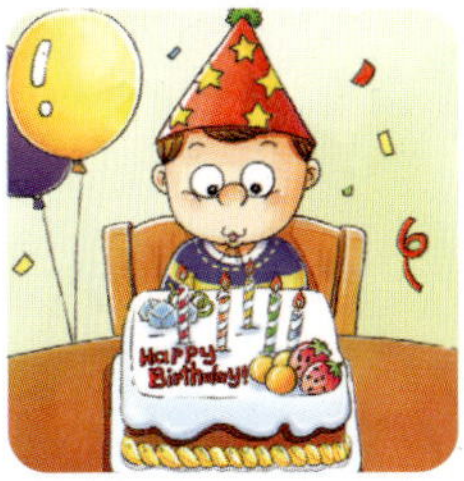

birthday

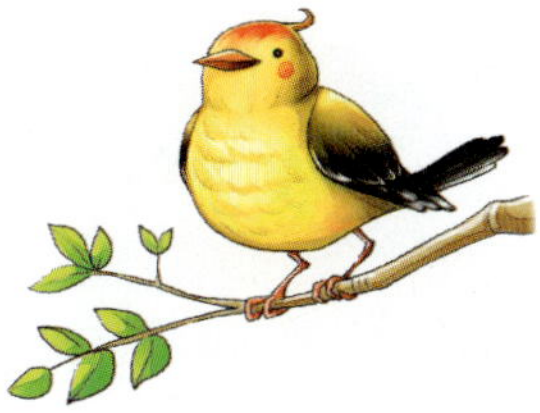

bird

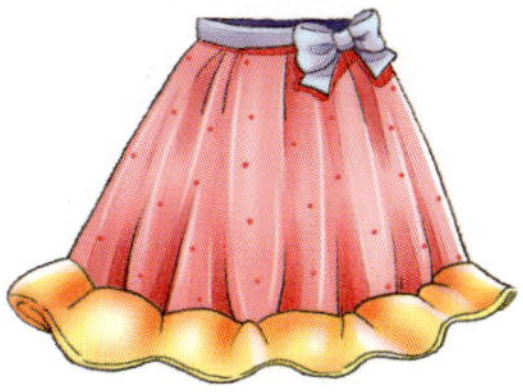

skirt

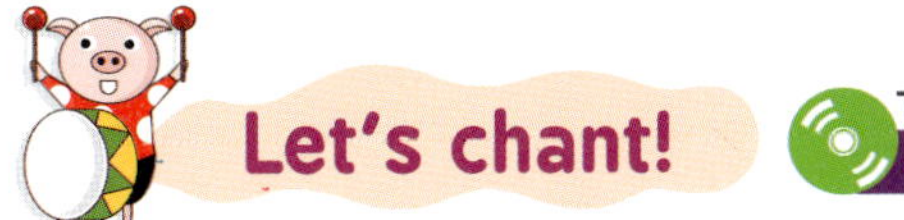

Let's chant! Track 78

Write the correct letters.

er   **ir**   **ur**

1

n____se

2

socc____

3

b____thday

4

lett____

5

g____l

6

p____se

7

sh____t

8

flow____

9

t____tle

Circle and write the word for the picture.

pursebirdturtlesoccerbirthdayshirtskirtdirtletter

1

2

3

4

5

6

7

8

9

Write the word in the correct column.

Listen, then circle the correct picture and double letters.

Listen and unscramble the letters. Then write the word.

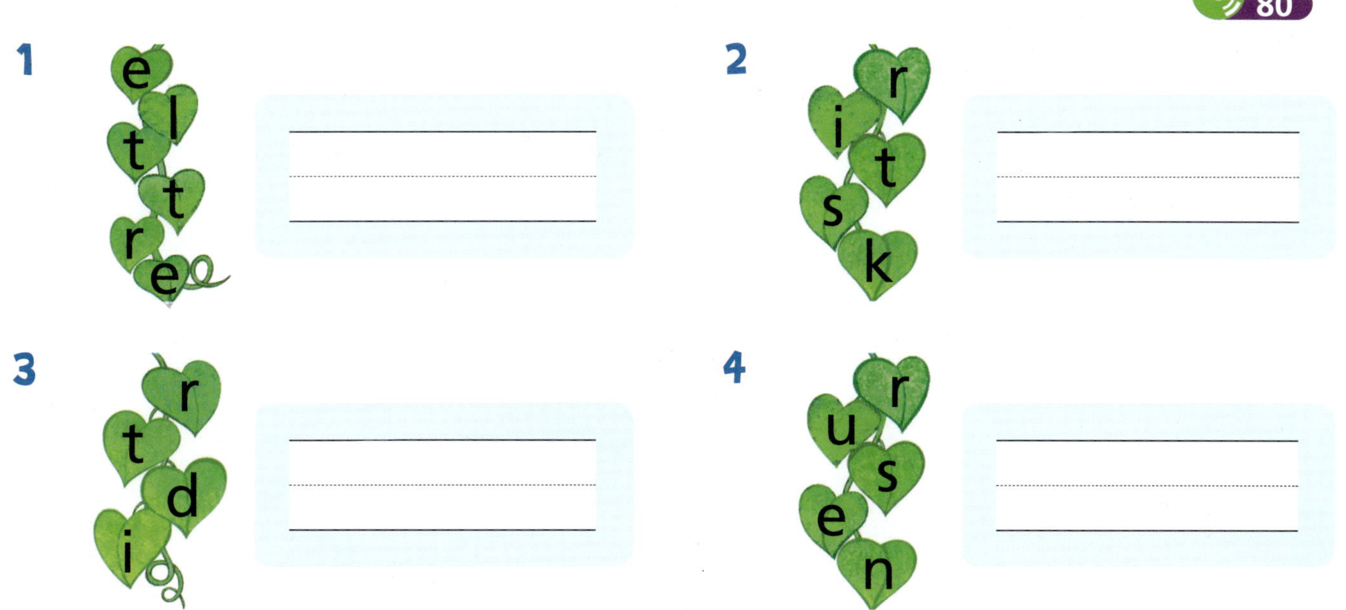

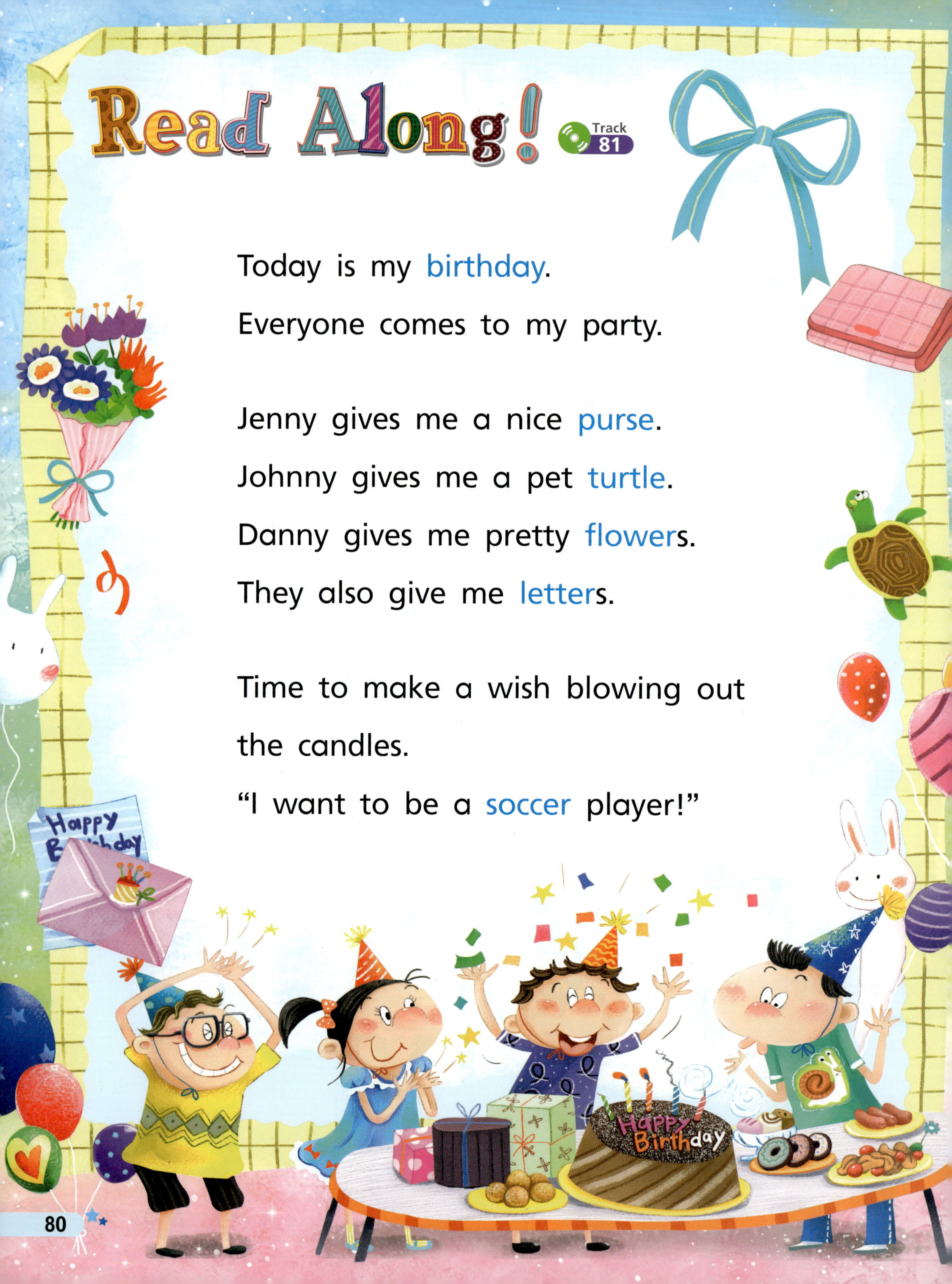

Read Along!

Today is my birthday.

Everyone comes to my party.

Jenny gives me a nice purse.

Johnny gives me a pet turtle.

Danny gives me pretty flowers.

They also give me letters.

Time to make a wish blowing out
the candles.

"I want to be a soccer player!"

Listen and write the correct word. 

1

A girl is wearing a yellow shirt and red

______________.

| bird | soccer | skirt |

2

There is a ______________ in the water.

| turtle | dirt | letter |

3

The man has a ______________ in the cage.

| birthday | soccer | bird |

4

Children are playing ______________ in the
playground.

| soccer | shirt | purse |

5

There is a green ______________ on the
table.

| purse | dirt | letter |

Connect the letters to complete the word.

1

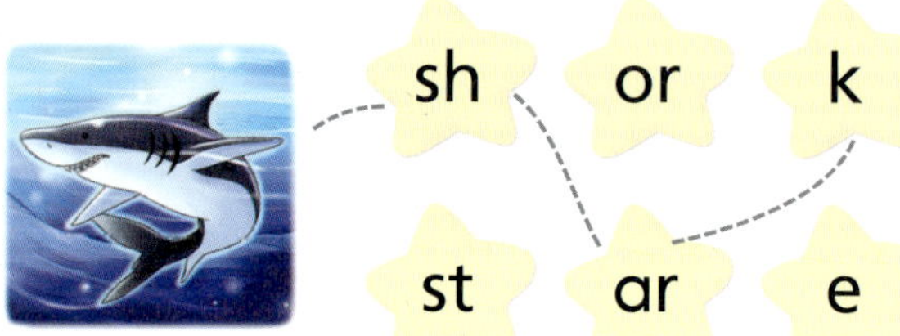

| sh | or | k |
| st | ar | e |

2

| le | tt | er |
| sk | ir | t |

3

| f | ar | d |
| c | or | k |

4

| n | ir | se |
| d | ur | t |

5

| r | ar | d |
| b | ir | k |

6

| g | or | n |
| h | ir | l |

7

| p | ar | s |
| n | ir | k |

8

| b | ir | n |
| d | ur | t |

Listen and circle the correct picture. Then complete the word. **Track 83**

Listen and unscramble the letters. Then match the correct picture. **Track 84**

1 mrafer → ________________ •

2 ccerso → ________________ •

3 tletur → ________________ •

4 thbirday → ________________ •

5 erots → ________________ •

6 drac → ________________ •

7 rtid → ________________ •

8 erusn → ________________ •

Listen and connect the correct words. Track 85

Listen and circle the picture.  Track 86

1 The woman buys the fresh  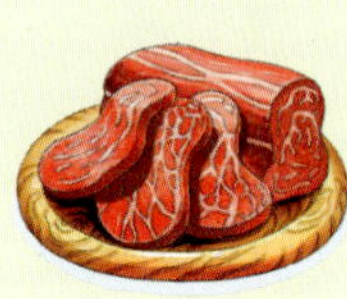  .

2 The boy is wearing a   shirt.

3 There is a    in a cage.

4 The children play in the    .

5 The man eats the food with a  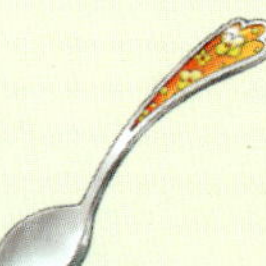  .

Listen to the word and circle the correct sound. Track 87

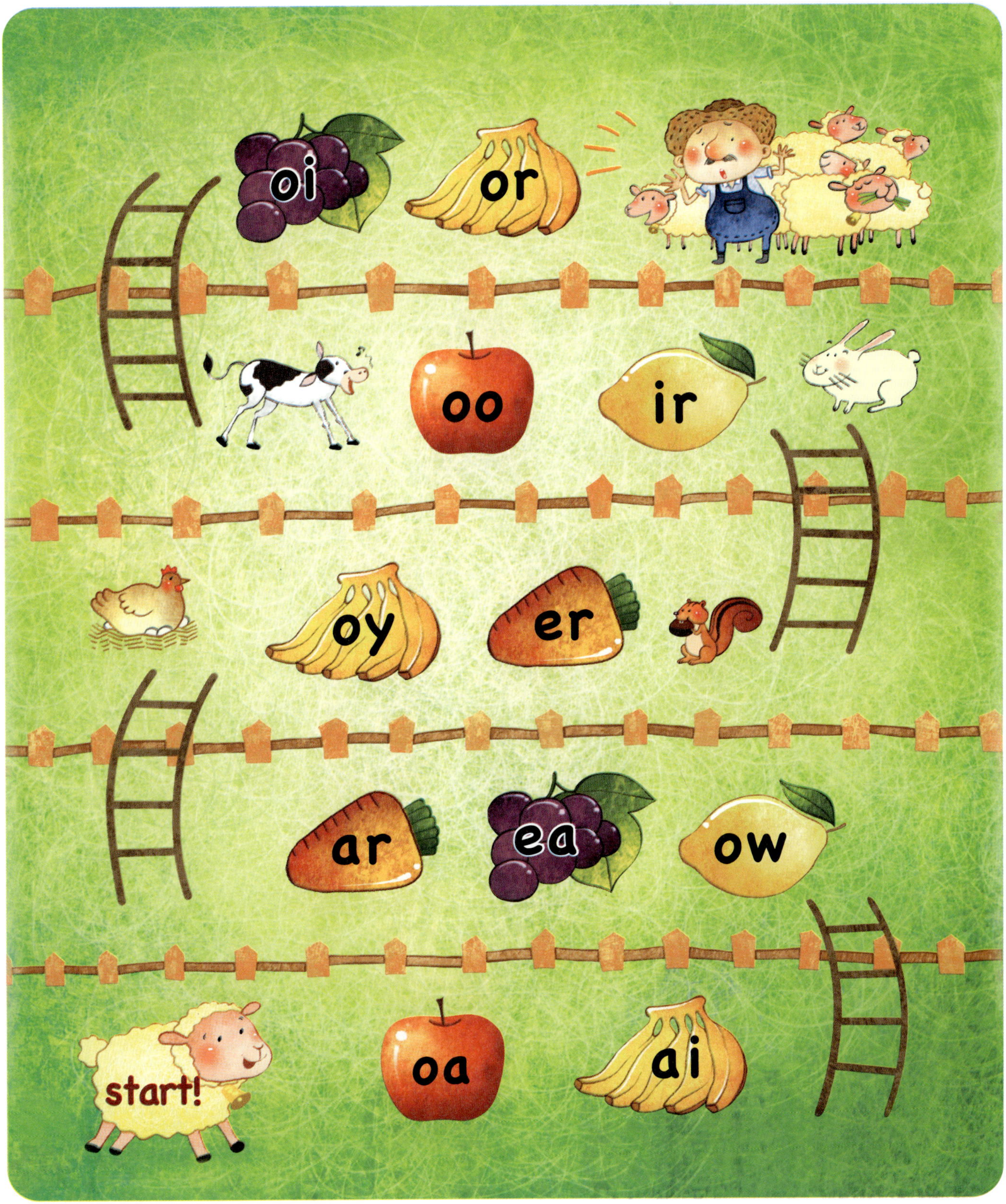

Match and write the word.

1 ee  **2** ou  **3** ay  **4** oo  **5** ar 

 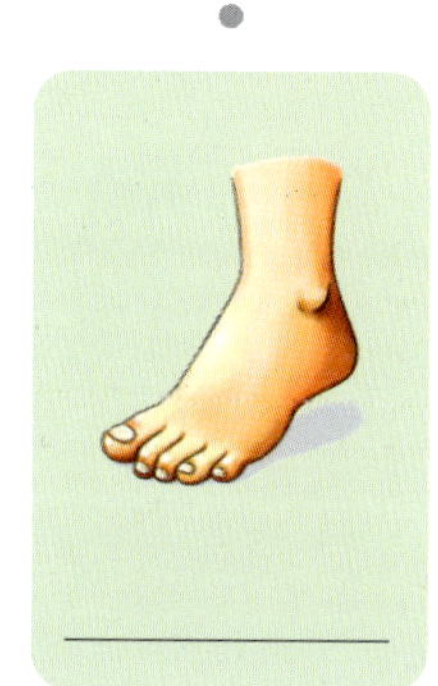   

6 oa  **7** ow 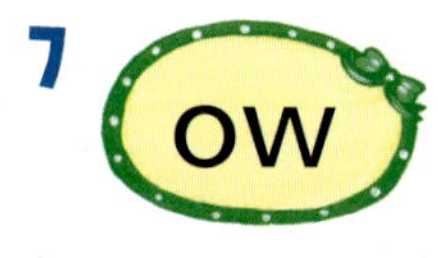 **8** oi  **9** ur 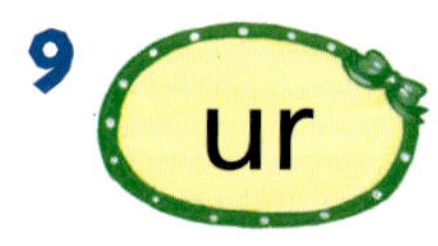 **10** er 

Check the correct sentence for the picture.

1

- ☐ The girl drinks tea on the terrace.
- ☐ The girl boils water on the stove.

2

- ☐ It snows heavily outside the window.
- ☐ It rains lightly outside the door.

3

- ☐ The man is looking at the moon.
- ☐ The man is looking at a star.

4

- ☐ The girl is wearing a gray skirt.
- ☐ The girl is wearing a green blouse.

5

- ☐ The boy gives the mail to the girl.
- ☐ The girl gives the book to the boy.

1

2

Mommy! Mommy! I can't sleep.

The **seal** from the **sea** cries waa, waa.

The **owl** from the **wood**s cries hoot, hoot.

Daddy! Daddy! I can't sleep.

The **goat** from the farm cries baa, baa.

The **goose** from the lake cries goggle, goggle.

✓ Check the pictures, referring to the words from the story.

 ✓     

3

Grandpa! Grandma! I can't sleep.

The **cow** from the barn cries moo, moo.

The **bird** from the **tree** cries chirp, chirp.

4

No dear, the **seal** and **owl** say good-night.

The **goat** and **goose** say sleep well.

The **cow** and **bird** say sweet dreams.

So, go to sleep now.

Let's play a game
oo (long)
oy
ea
ou
oa
Start
oy
oo (short)
Jump up and down 3 times.
oi
ar
ai
ee
or
ow (cow)
ow (row)
ir
How to play
Step 1 Roll the die and go to the correct number of spaces. Say the word with the given letters.
Step 2 If you land on the space with a sentence, read it and follow the instruction.
Step 3 If you get to the 'Finish' first, you win this game.

oo (short)
ea
ee
ur
oa
ou
er
Clap your hands 5 times.
or
oi
ar
oi
ee
oo (long)
ur
ir
ou
ay
ow (cow)
ou
ay
Do a dance!
ai
Finish
ow (row)
oy
er
93

Final Test

Listen to the word and check the correct word. **Track 89**

e.g.

 ❶ soap  toast ❸ goat

1

 ❶ ground ❷ south  ❸ cloud

2

 ❶ train ❷ tail ❸ mail

3

 ❶ north ❷ horse ❸ store

4

 ❶ oyster ❷ joy ❸ royal

5

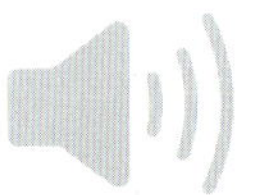 ❶ tree ❷ feet ❸ peel

Listen to the word and check the correct number for the picture.

e.g. ✓ ① ② ③

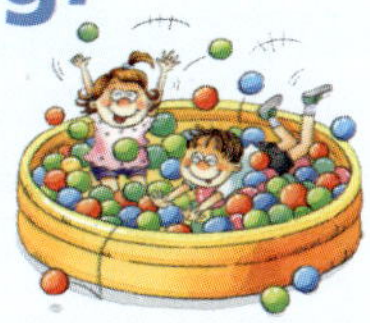

6 ① ② ③

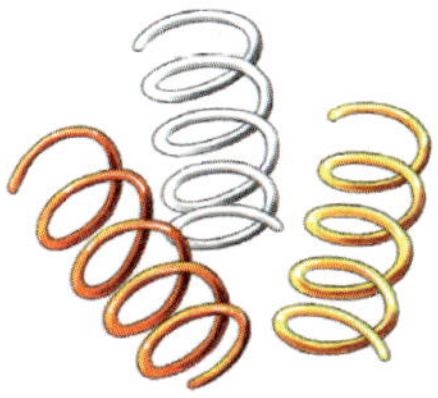

7 ① ② ③

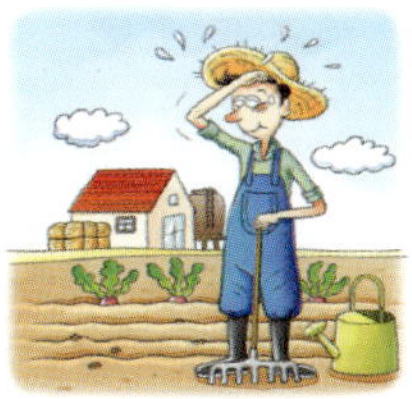

8 ① ② ③

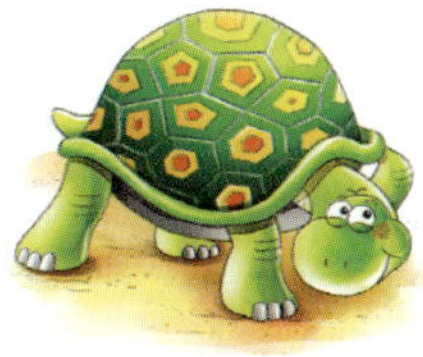

9 ① ② ③

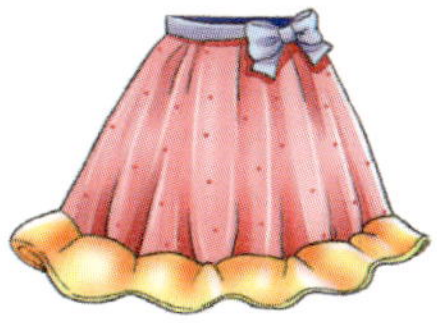

10 ① ② ③

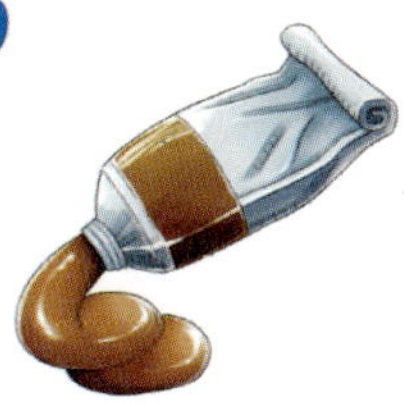

Listen to the word and write the missing letters. Track 91

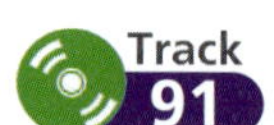

e.g.

s	o	c	c	e	r

11

s			p

12

m			t

13

s	n		

14

r			a	l

15

t	r		

16

s			t	h

17

w			d

18

s	t			e

19

p	l		

20

s	h			k

Check the correct word for the picture.

e.g.   ✔ ① rail   ② mail   ③ rain

21    ① hay   ② play   ③ May

22    ① seed   ② peel   ③ green

23    ① tea   ② leaf   ③ peanut

24    ① dirt   ② birthday   ③ bird

25    ① window   ② toast   ③ mouse

Check the correct picture with the given letters.

e.g. ee

26 ay

27 oa

28 oi

29 oo

30 ow

Choose and write the correct words.

e.g.

The _farmer_ has some _soybean_ s.

soybean   goose   farmer   hook

31

The children __________ at the __________.

row   moon   soil   look

32

A __________ on the rock is in the __________.

rain   tree   south   seal

33

A __________ is feeding on __________.

crown   foot   hay   horse

34

There are many __________s in front of the __________.

store   soap   tray   flower

Glossary

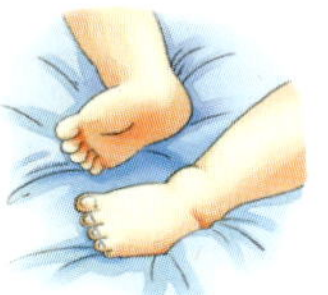

bee   tree   feet   tea   sea   seal

seed   peel   green   leaf   meat   peanut

Unit 2 | **ai · ay**

rain   mail   train   gray   clay   hay

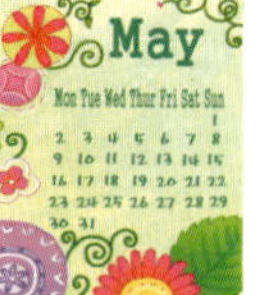

nail   rail   tail   play   tray   May

Unit 3 | oa · ow

 coat

 boat

 soap

 bowl

 row

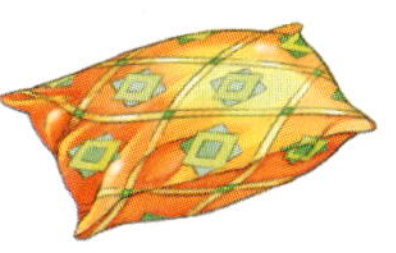 pillow

 road

 goat

 toast

 window

 snow

 yellow

Unit 4 | oi · oy

 coin

 boil

 soil

 toy

 boy

 oyster

 oil

 foil

 coil

 joy

soybean

 royal

Glossary

Unit 5 | ou · ow

 mouse

 cloud

 house

 cow

 owl

 brown

 south

 ground

 blouse

 clown

 crown

 gown

Unit 6 | oo

 moon

 spoon

 root

 book

 cook

 wood

 goose

 pool

 broom

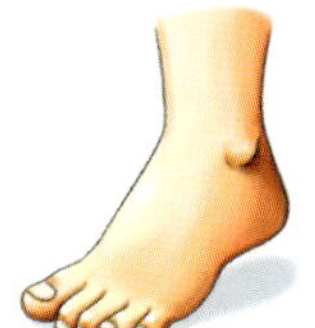 foot

 hook

 look

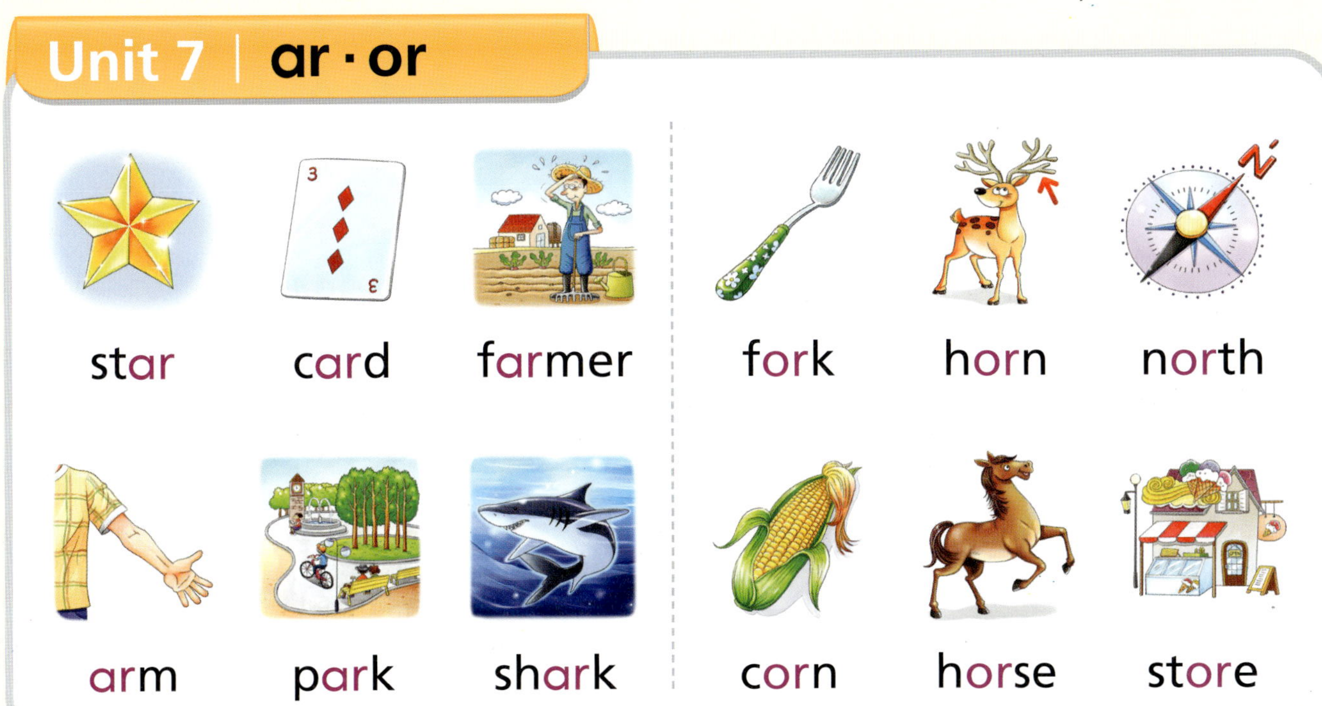

star · card · farmer · fork · horn · north

arm · park · shark · corn · horse · store

flower · letter · soccer · girl · dirt · shirt

purse · nurse · turtle · birthday · bird · skirt

Phonics
wonder

Phonics Wonder

LEVEL 5

Double Letter Vowels

Workbook

Phonics Wonder

LEVEL 5

Double Letter Vowels

Workbook

YSG Young & Son Global, Inc.

Contents

ee ea

Look and circle the correct letters.

1) 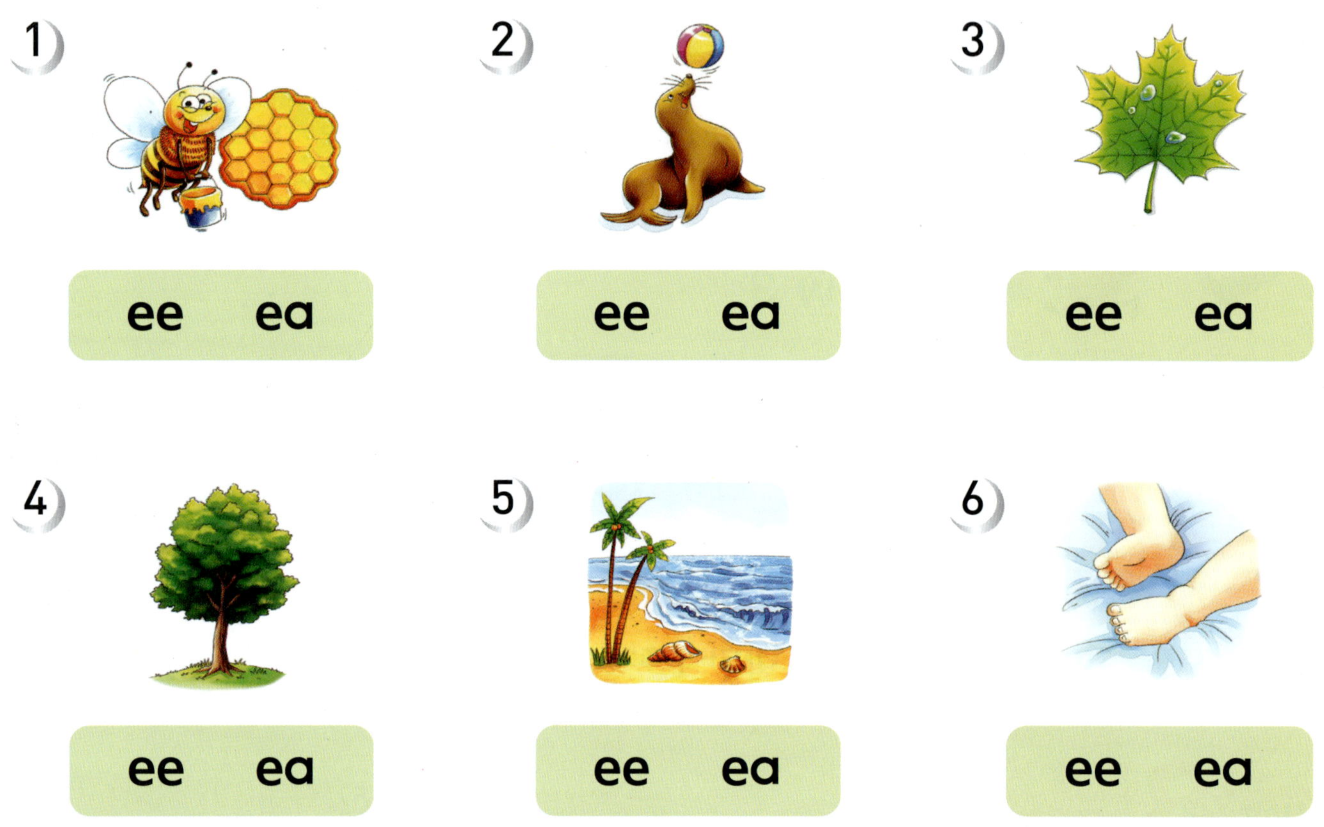

ee   ea

2) ee   ea

3) ee   ea

4) ee   ea

5) ee   ea

6) ee   ea

Trace and read.

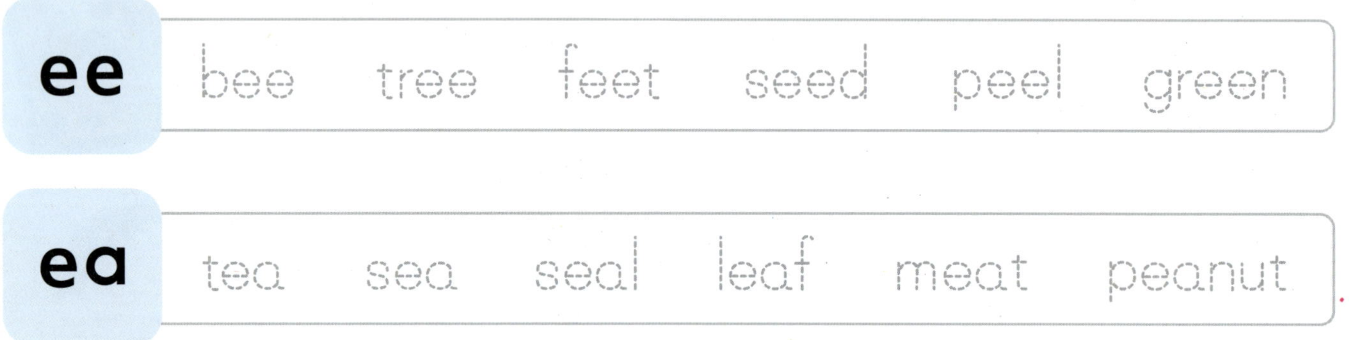

ee	bee tree feet seed peel green
ea	tea sea seal leaf meat peanut

Match and complete the word.

1

2

3

4

5

6

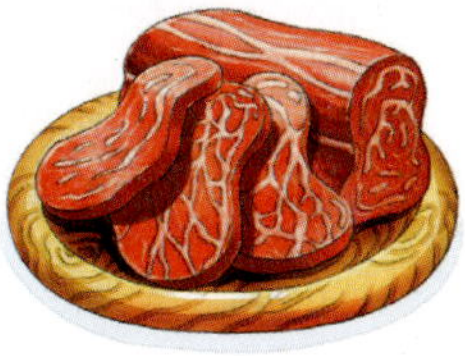

ee

ea

s   d

gr   n

p   l

p   nut

t

m   t

Circle the correct picture.

1 bee

2 feet

3 leaf

4 meat

5 green

6 tea

7 sea

8 seed

ee

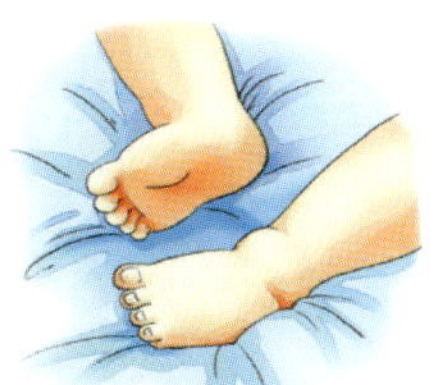  

___________ ___________ ___________

___________ ___________ ___________

ea

  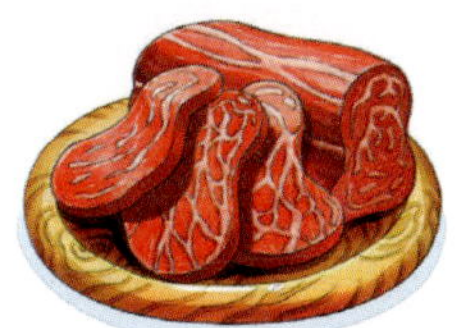

___________ ___________ ___________

___________ ___________ ___________

ai ay

Look and circle the correct letters.

1)  ai ay

2) ai ay

3) ai ay

4) ai ay

5) ai ay

6) ai ay

Trace and read.

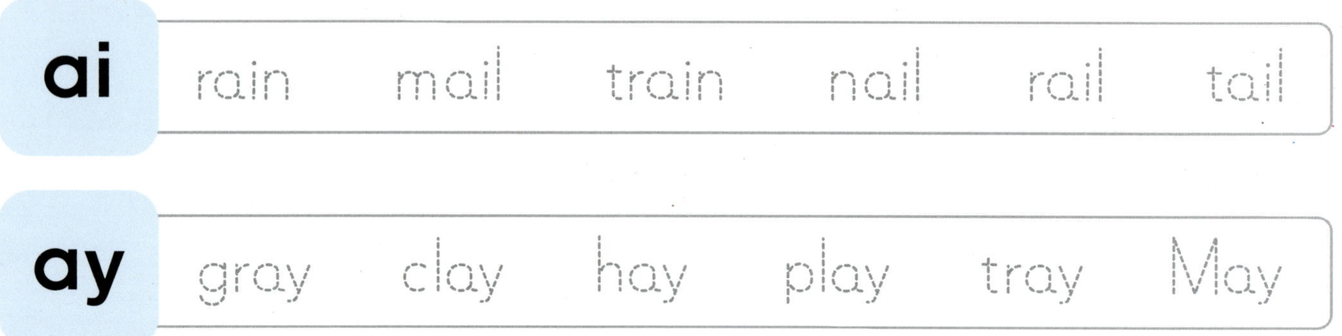

| **ai** | rain | mail | train | nail | rail | tail |

| **ay** | gray | clay | hay | play | tray | May |

Match and complete the word.

1

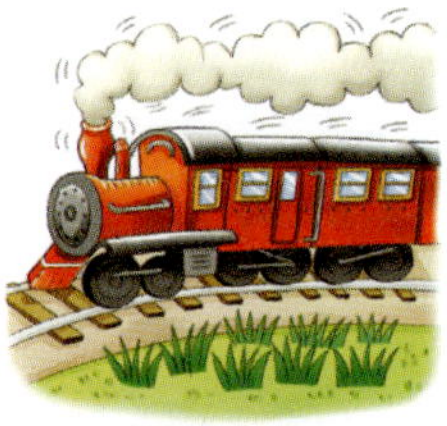

2

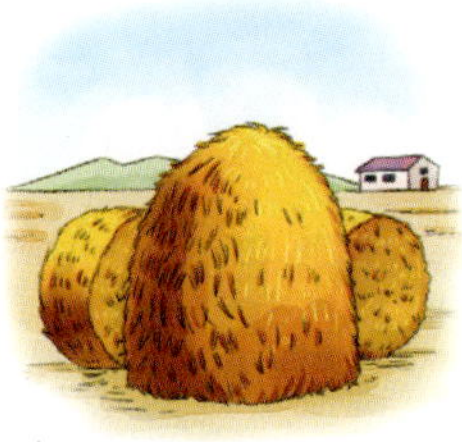

3

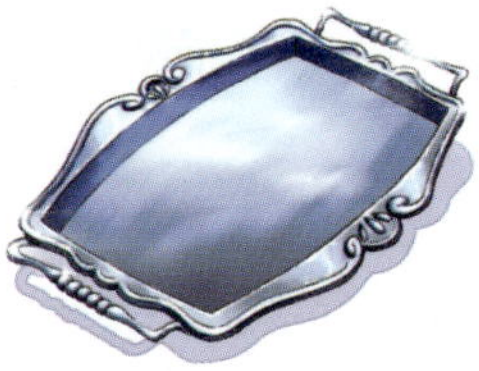

4

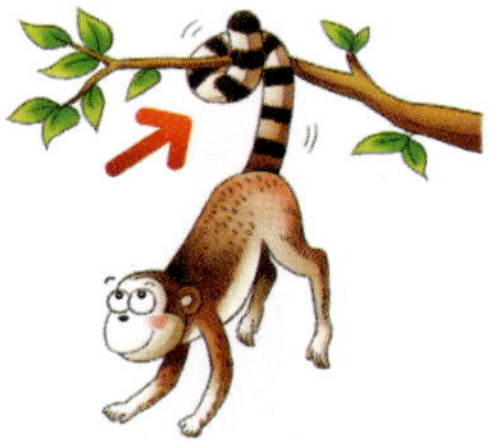

5

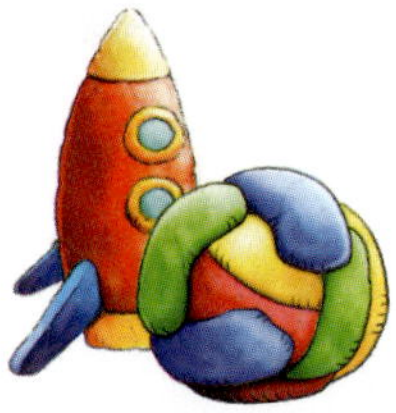

6

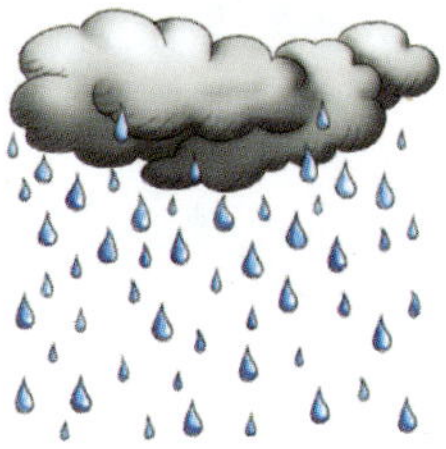

Circle the correct picture.

Write the word.

ai

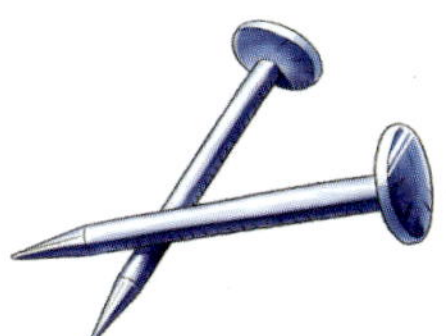  

ay

  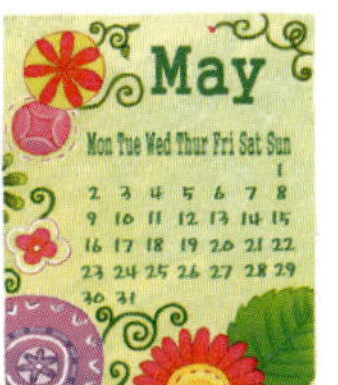

Circle the picture with the same vowel letters as the first picture.

1

  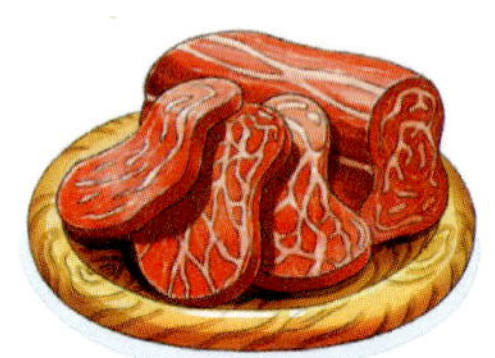 

2

 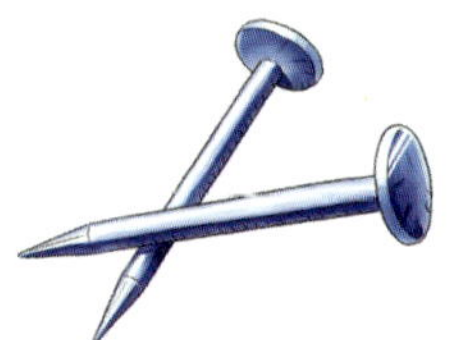  

3

4

 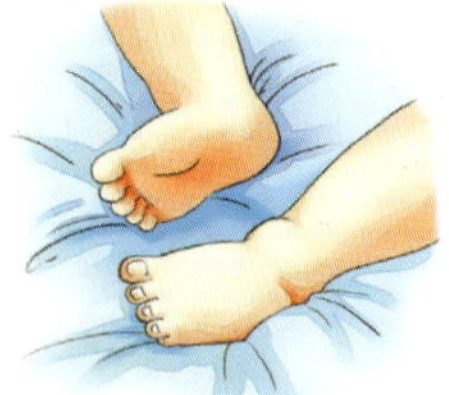  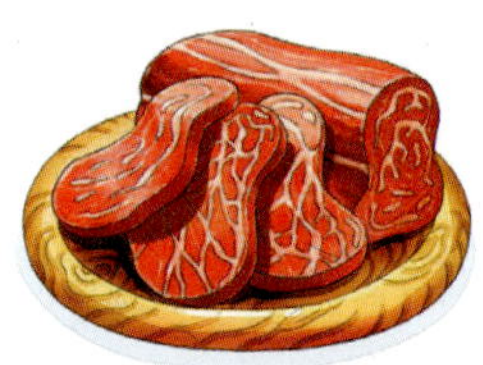

5

Circle the correct word for the picture.

1 

peel leaf bee

2 

nail train May

3 

tea rail hay

4 

gray bee seal

5 

seed tray mail

6 

tree clay rain

7 

sea peel play

8 

meat green tail

9 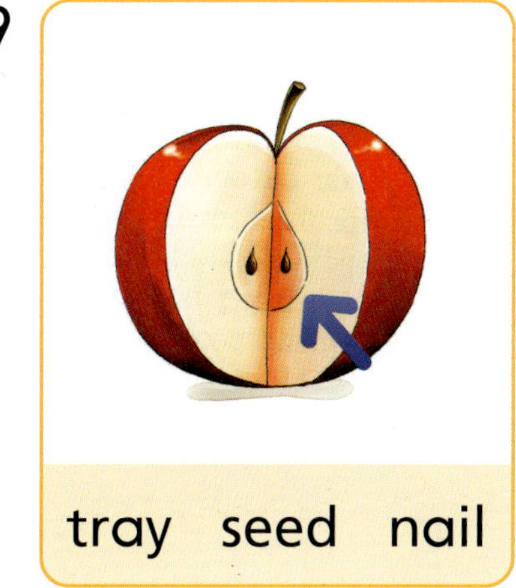

tray seed nail

Choose and write the correct letters for the picture.

| ee | ea | ai | ay |

Find and circle the word for each picture. Then write it.

p e t b e e r y u t r a y h u m e a t f

1

2

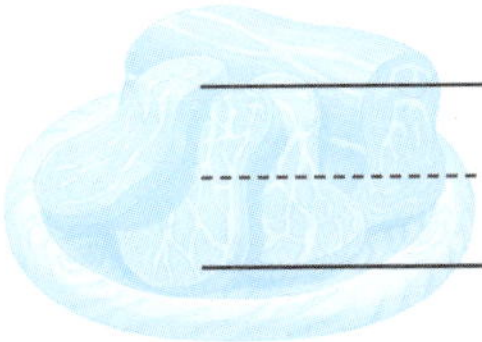

3

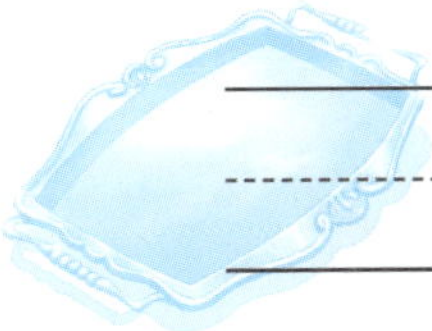

h q p l a y r c v l f e e t d s r a i l

4

5

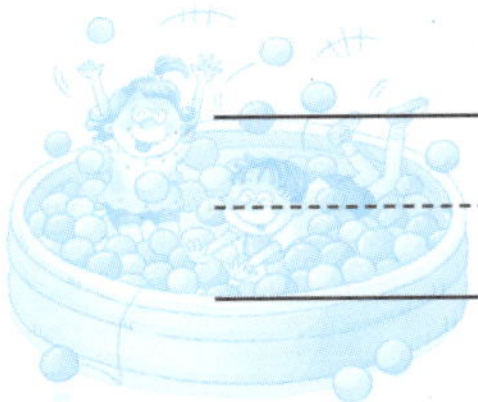

6

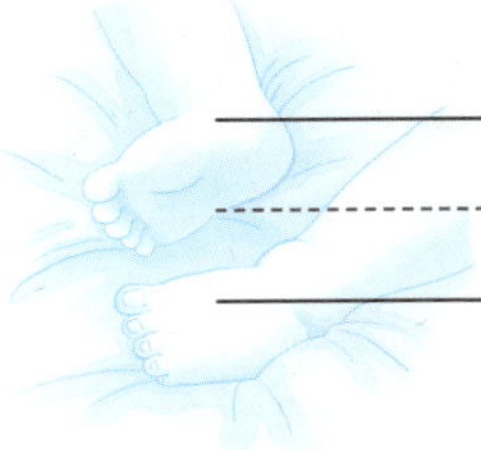

s e a r r w y l e a f a s h t r a i n f

7

8

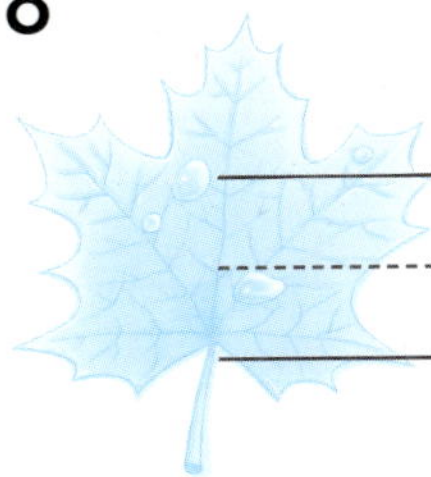

9

oa ow

Connect the picture with the correct letters.

1   2   3   4

oa

ow

5   6   7   8

Trace and read.

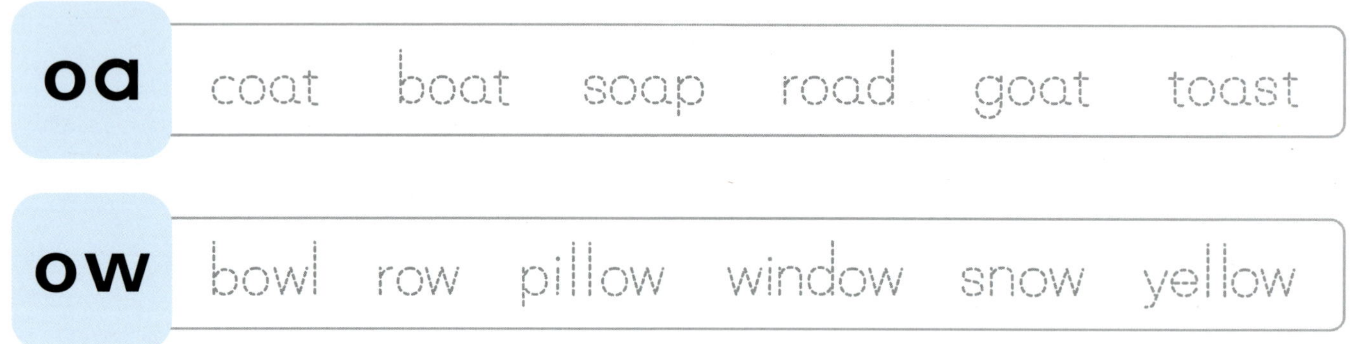

oa	coat boat soap road goat toast
ow	bowl row pillow window snow yellow

Unscramble the letters and write the word.

1 ye ow ll ________________

2 n s ow ________________

3 ow r ________________

4 s p oa ________________

5 oa t b ________________

6 st oa t ________________

Circle the correct word.

1 
row | soap

2 
pillow | goat

3 
road | window

4 
soap | bowl

5 
bowl | goat

6 
snow | window

7 
soap | row

8 
toast | snow

Write the word.

oa

ow

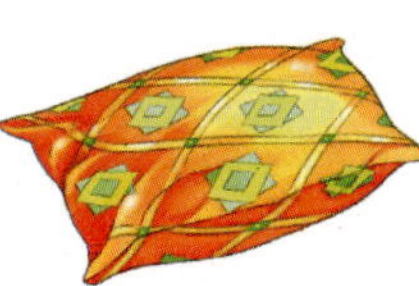  

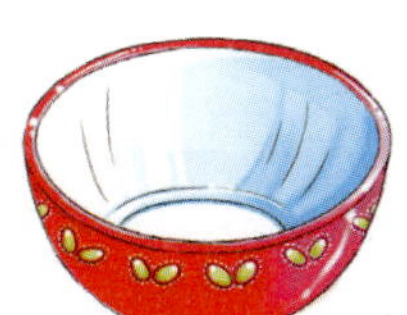  

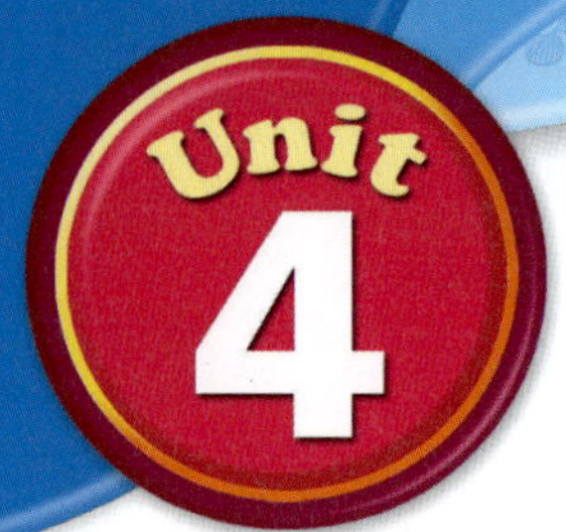

Unit 4 oi oy

Connect the picture with the correct letters.

1 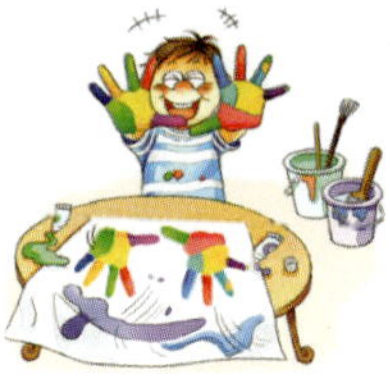

5 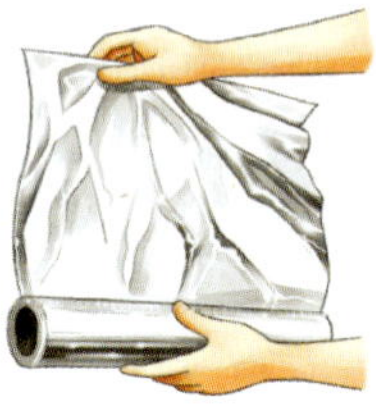

2 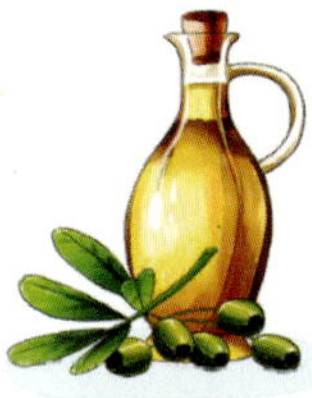

oi

6 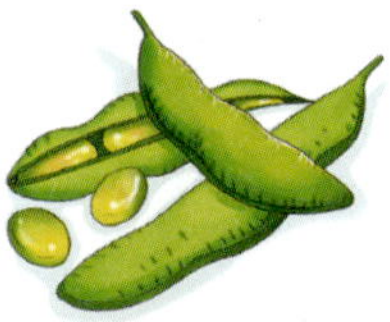

3 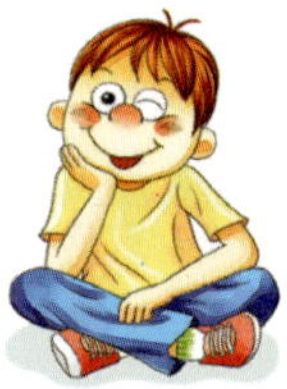

oy

7 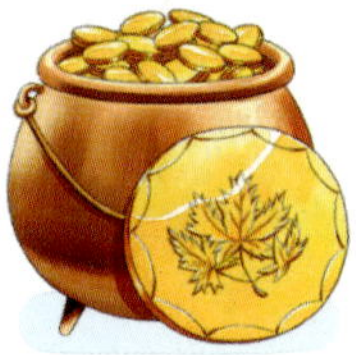

4 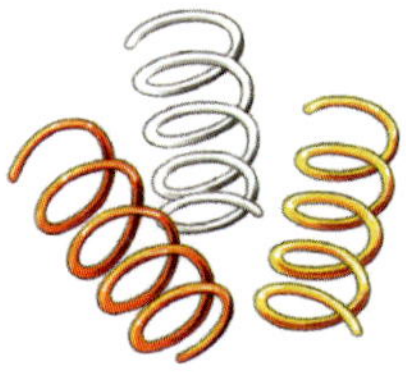

8 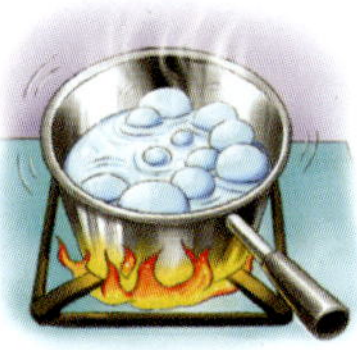

Trace and read.

oi	coin boil soil oil foil coil
oy	toy boy oyster joy soybean royal

Unscramble the letters and write the word.

1   oi   s   l   ______________

2   er   oy   st   ______________

3   c   n   oi   ______________

4   al   r   oy   ______________

5   l   b   oi   ______________

6   oy   t   ______________

Circle the correct word.

1

soil | coin

2

joy | foil

3

coin | royal

4

royal | foil

5

soybean | boil

6

oil | joy

7

foil | toy

8
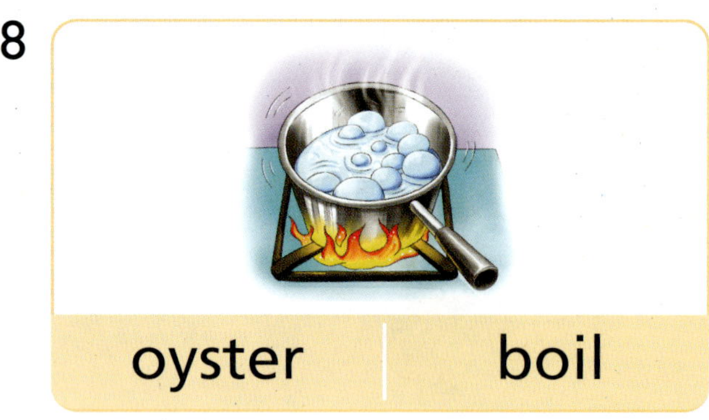
oyster | boil

Write the word.

oi

oy

Circle the picture with the same vowel letters as the first picture.

1    

2    

3    

4    

5    

Circle the correct word for the picture.

1 row road boy

2 coat oil snow

3 boil bowl joy

4 boy goat toy

5 boat soap mail

6 pillow foil coat

7 toast coil yellow

8 royal window soil

9 oyster coin row

Choose and write the correct letters for the picture.

oa   oi   ow   oy

Find and circle. Then write the word.

r	o	y	a	l	b
o	o	a	z	t	o
w	o	a	i	s	y
w	i	n	d	o	w
m	l	a	p	a	x
s	o	i	l	p	z

1 

2 

3 

4 

________________ ________________ ________________ ________________

5 

6 

7 

8 

________________ ________________ ________________ ________________

Unit 5 ou ow

Look and circle the correct letters.

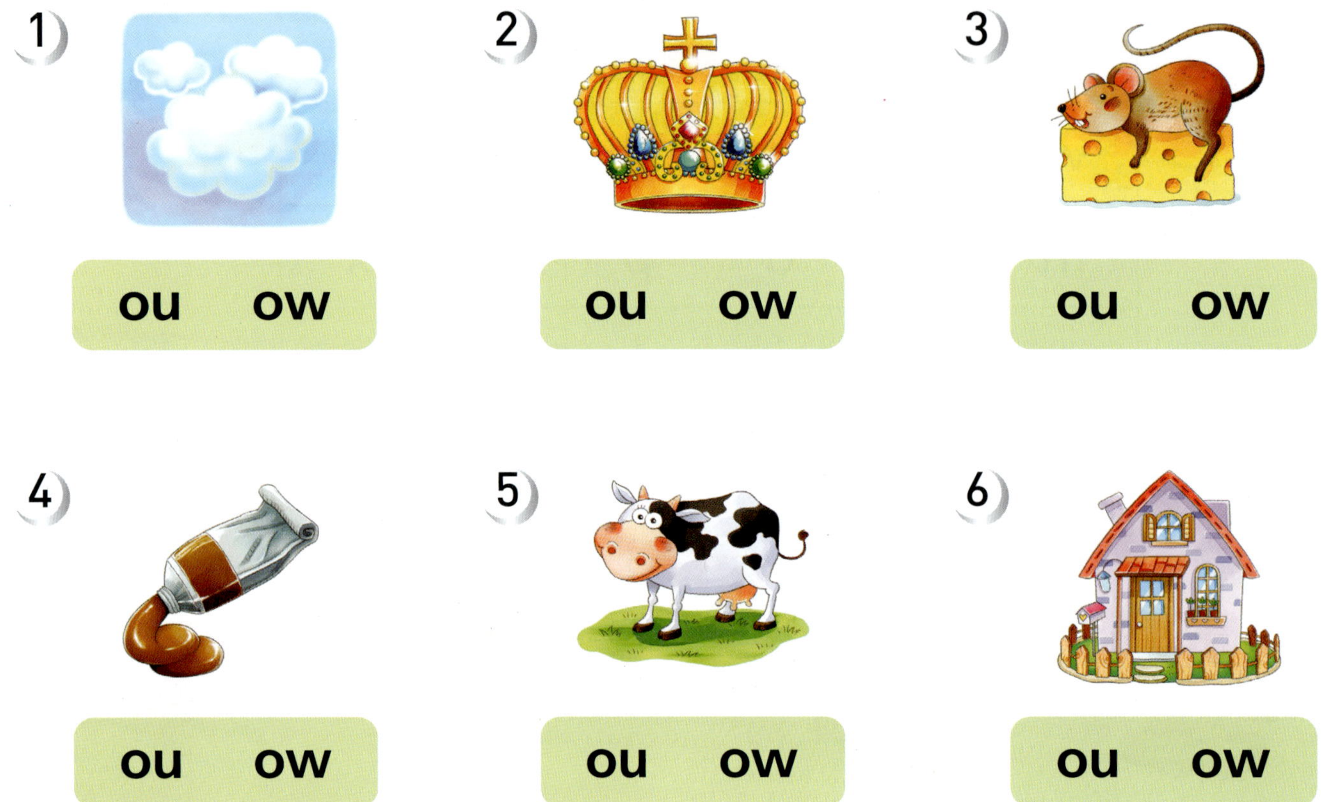

1)

ou ow

2)

ou ow

3)

ou ow

4)

ou ow

5)

ou ow

6)

ou ow

Trace and read.

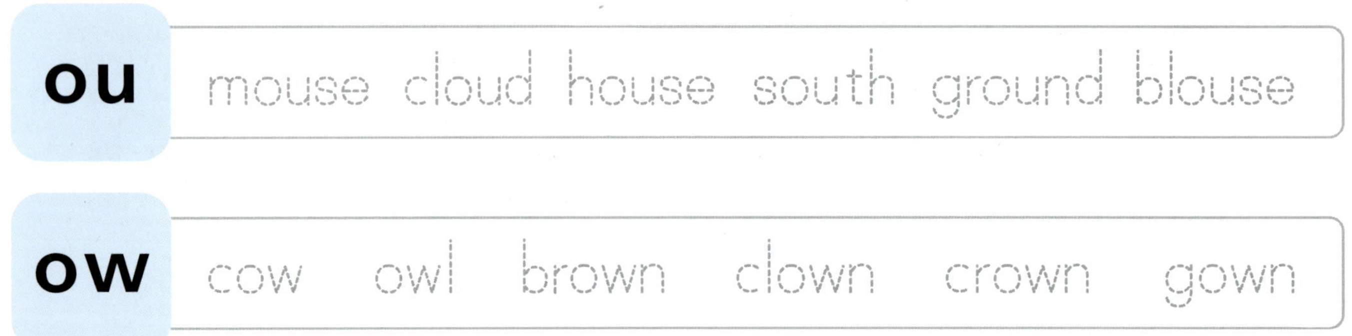

ou	mouse cloud house south ground blouse
ow	cow owl brown clown crown gown

Unscramble the letters and write the word.

1

(h / ou / se)

____

2

(n / ow / cl)

____

3

(ou / nd / gr)

____

4

(s / th / ou)

____

5

(ow / n / g)

____

6

(ow / c)

____

7

(se / ou / bl)

____

8

(ow / l)

____

9

(ou / m / se)

____

Circle the correct picture.

1 house

2 gown

3 crown

4 south

5 ground

6 cloud

7 cow

8 brown

ou

ow

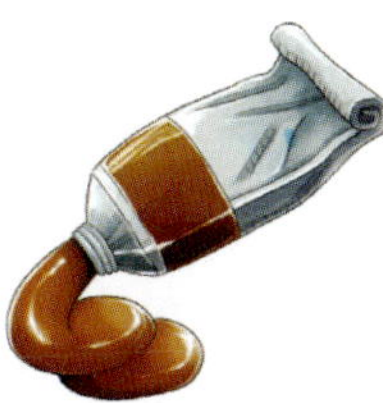  

Unit 6 — oo

Connect the picture with the correct letters.

1 
5
2
6
oo (long)
3
7
oo (short)
4
8

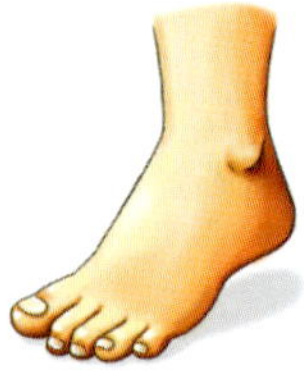

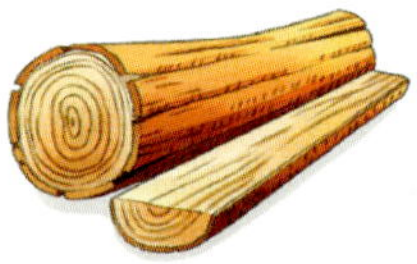

Trace and read.

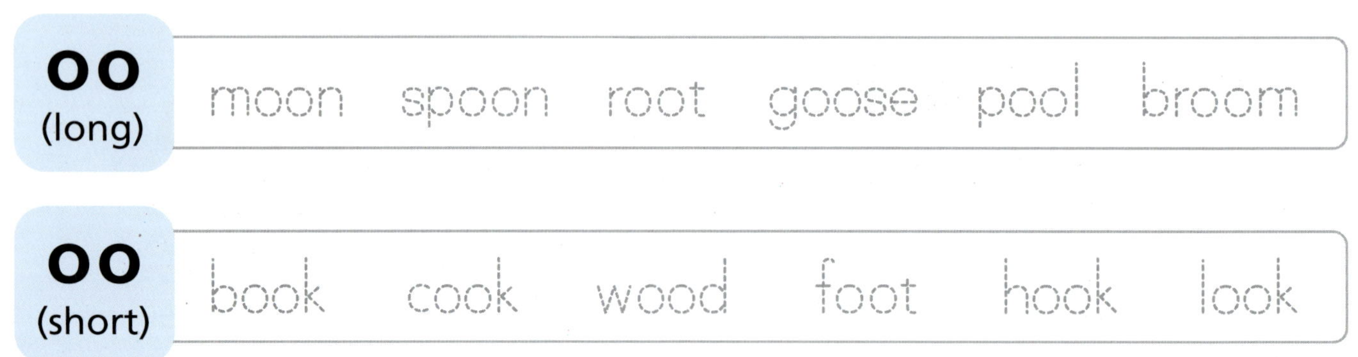

oo (long)
moon   spoon   root   goose   pool   broom

oo (short)
book   cook   wood   foot   hook   look

Unscramble the letters and write the word.

1 

(h / oo / k)

____

2 

(n / oo / sp)

____

3 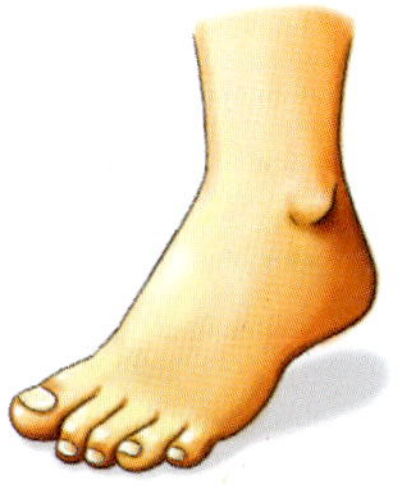

(t / oo / f)

____

4 

(oo / n / m)

____

5 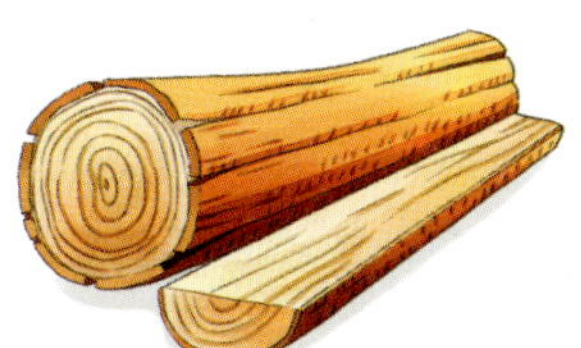

(d / oo / w)

____

6 

(r / t / oo)

____

7 

(c / oo / k)

____

8 

(m / oo / br)

____

9 

(b / k / oo)

____

Circle the correct picture.

Write the word.

oo
(long)

oo
(short)

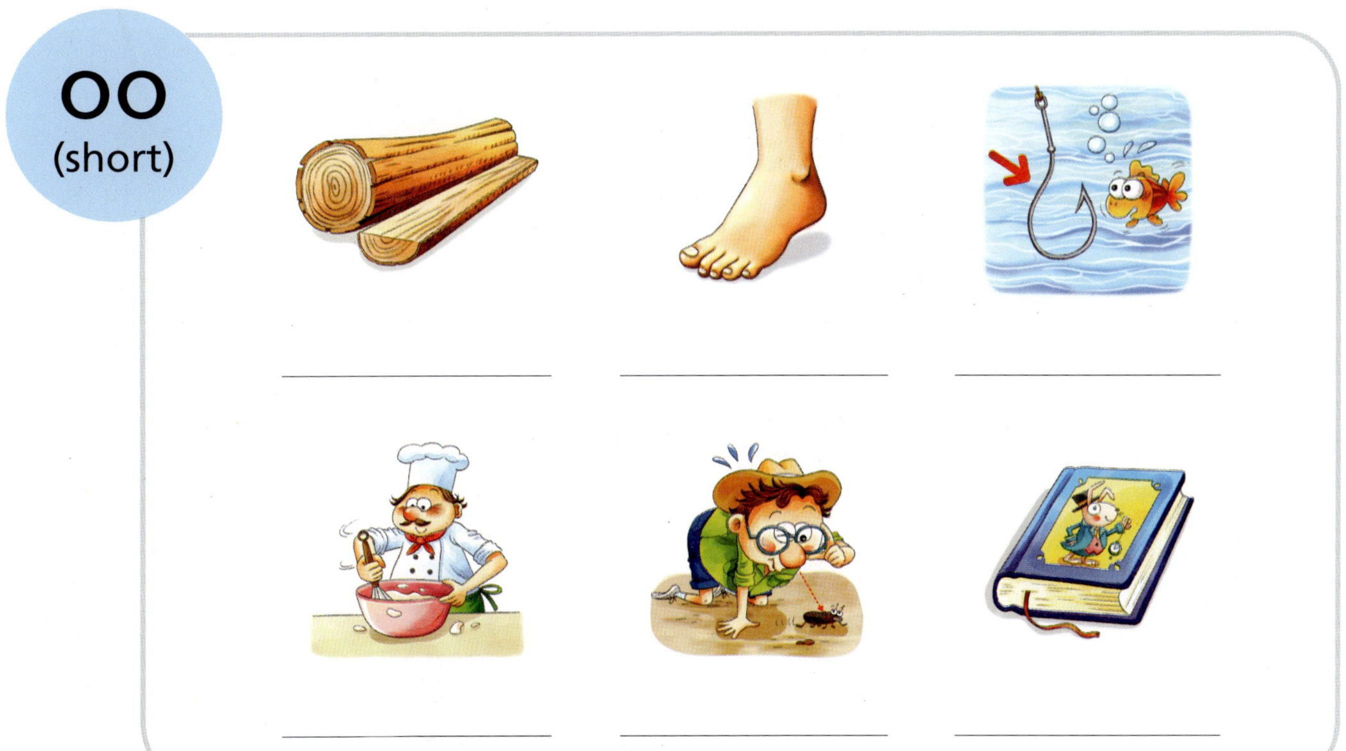

Circle the picture with the same vowel letters as the first picture.

1    

2 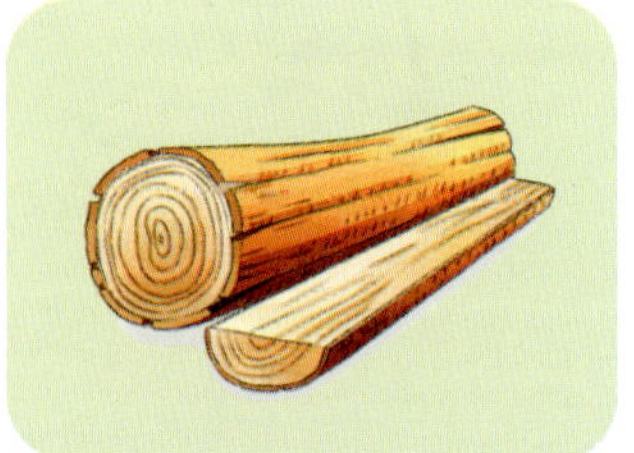   

3    

4    

5    

Circle the correct word for the picture.

1 

cow cloud root

2 

gown hook pool

3

owl ground look

4

house clown pool

5 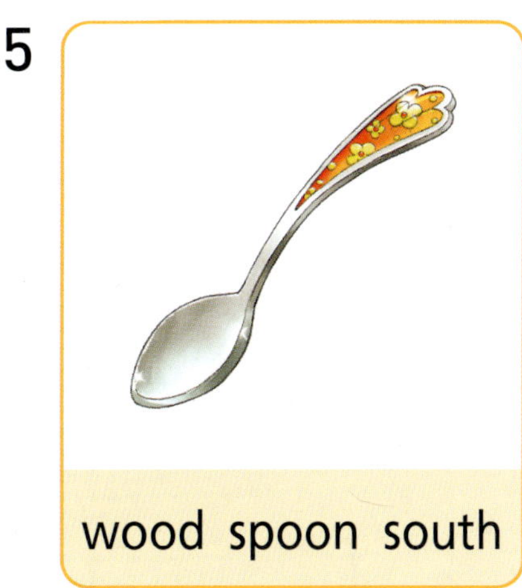

wood spoon south

6 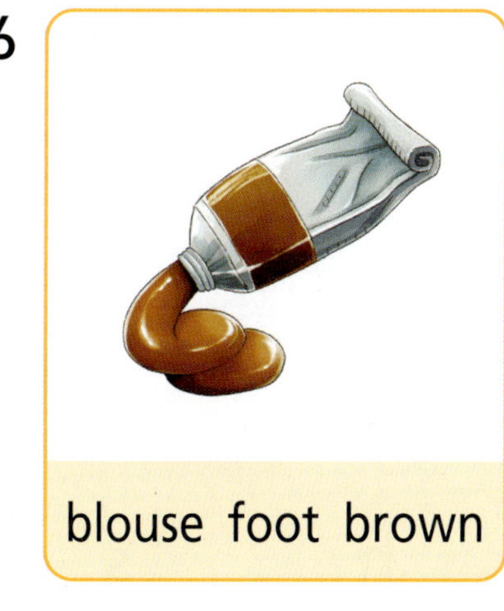

blouse foot brown

7

goose cook owl

8 

root crown hook

9 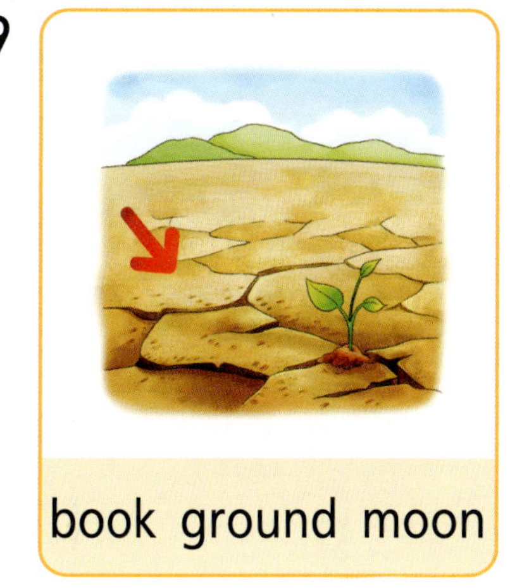

book ground moon

Choose and write the correct letters for the picture.

ou ow oo

1) g r _ _ n d

2) c _ _

3) g _ _ s e

4) h _ _ s e

5) f _ _ t

6) b r _ _ n

7) p _ _ l

8) c l _ _ d

9) h _ _ k

Find and circle the word for each picture. Then write it.

j e c u r o w y u c o i n h o c o a t f

1

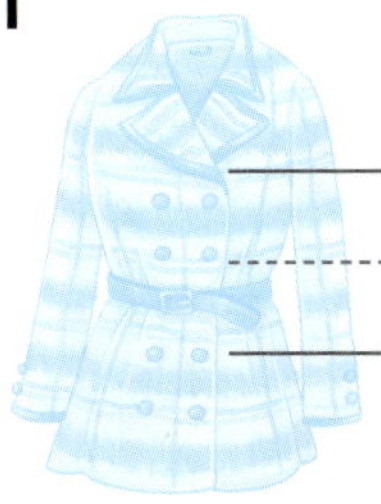

2

3

h q p b o i l c s g o a t t r o y a l t

4

5

6

s o a p d w s n o w l e s h l e f o i l

7

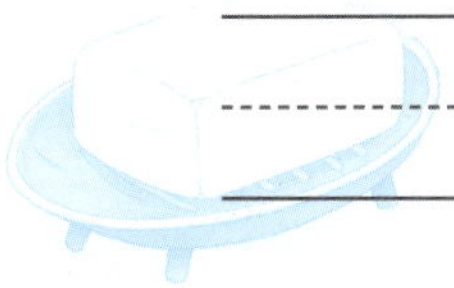

8

9

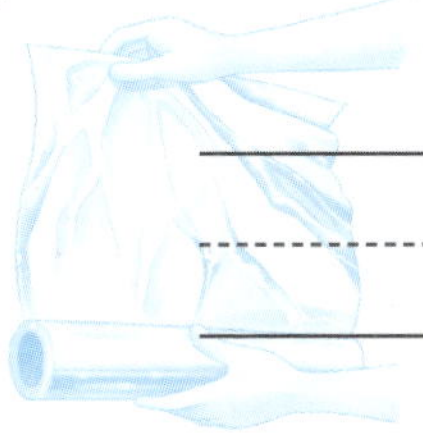

Circle the correct picture.

1   or

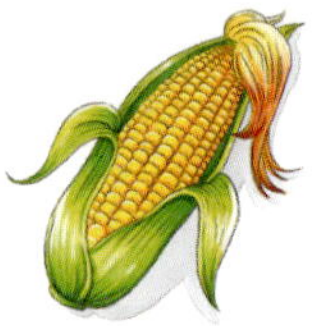

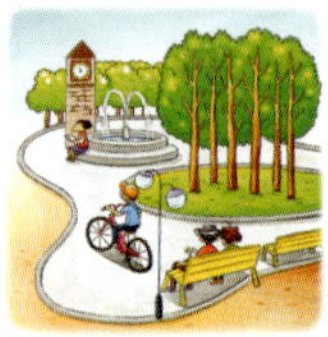

2   ar

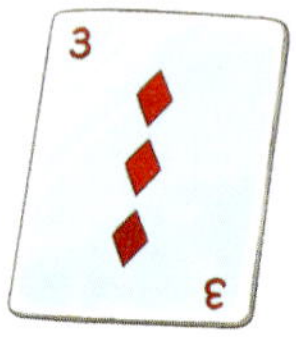

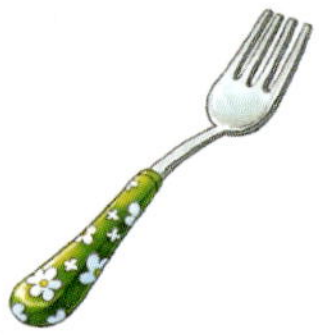

3   or

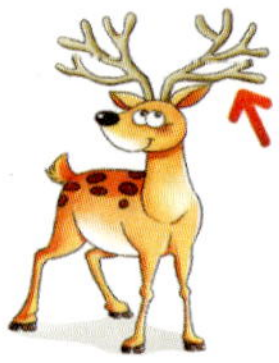

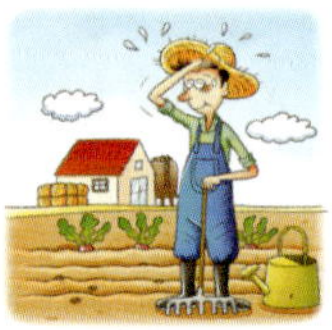

4   ar

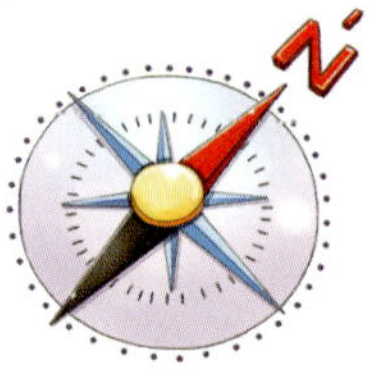

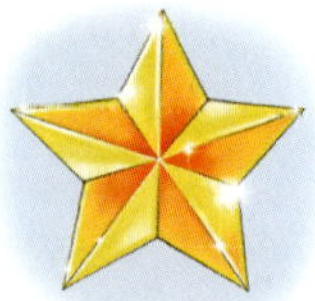

5   ar

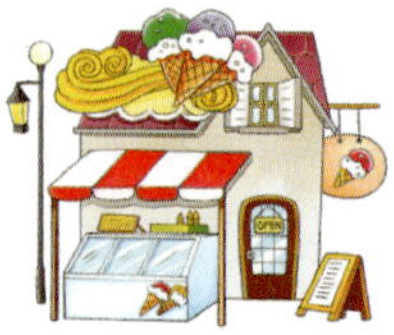

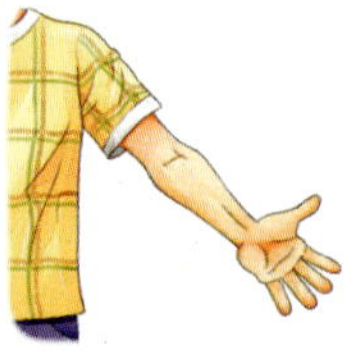

6   or

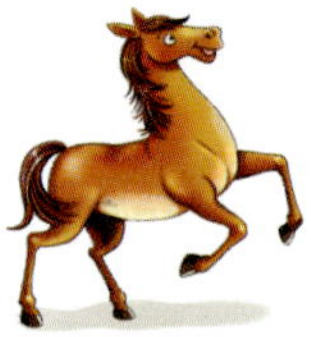

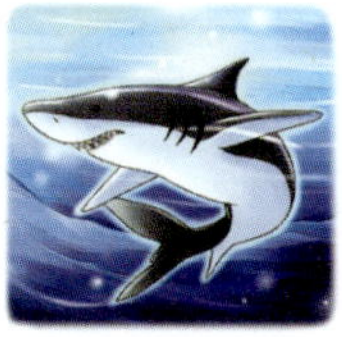

Trace and read.

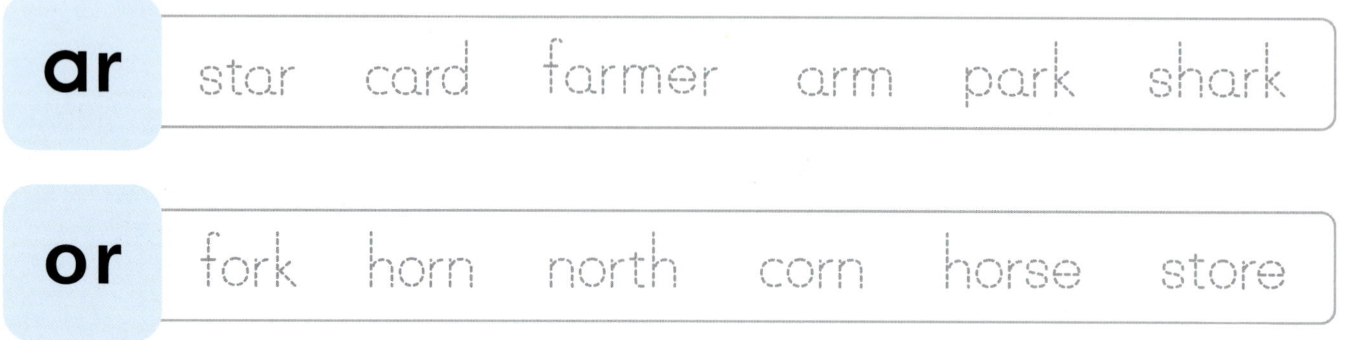

ar   star   card   farmer   arm   park   shark

or   fork   horn   north   corn   horse   store

Match and write the word.

1

2

3

4

5

6

ar

or

Circle the correct word.

1
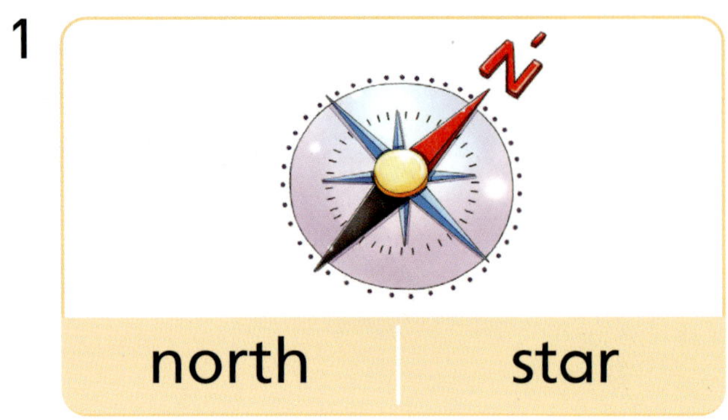
north | star

2

farmer | corn

3

arm | fork

4

horn | card

5

store | park

6

horse | shark

7

corn | star

8

store | park

Write the word.

ar

  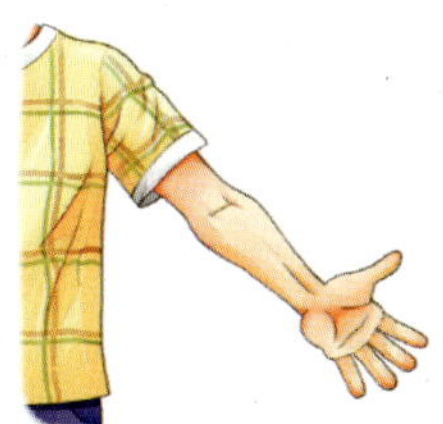

or

er ur ir

Look and circle the correct letters.

1)   **ir**   er

2)   **er**   ur

3)   **ur**   ir

4)   **er**   ir

5)   **ur**   er

6)   **ir**   ur

Trace and read.

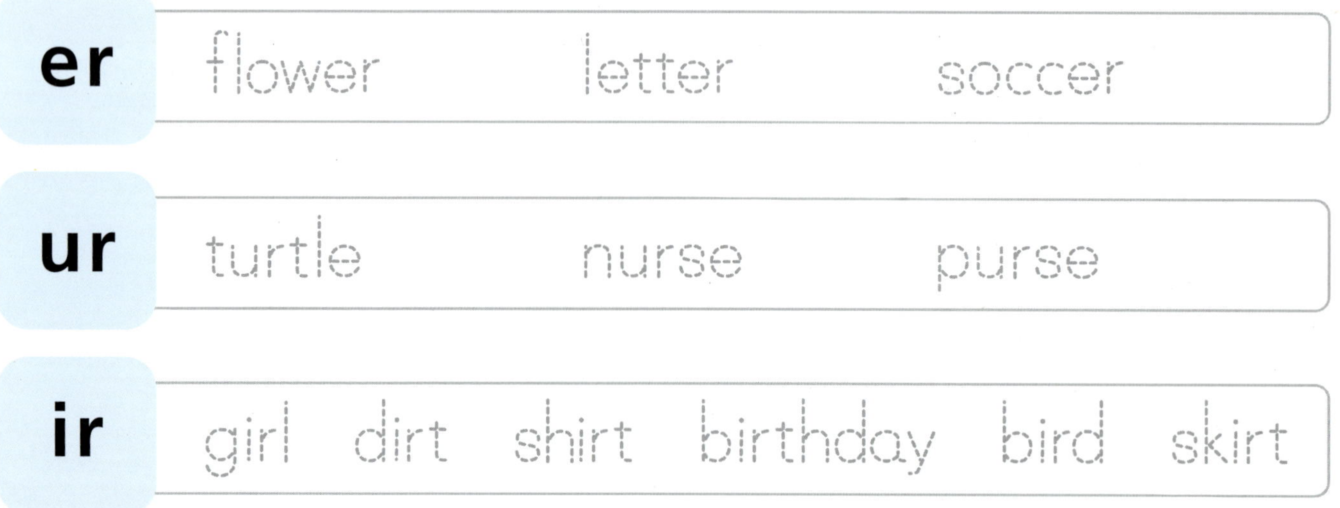

er	flower	letter	soccer
ur	turtle	nurse	purse
ir	girl dirt shirt birthday bird skirt		

Unscramble the letters and write the word.

1   fl er ow ______________

2   ur n se ______________

3   cc so er ______________

4   ir l g ______________

5   d b ir ______________

6   d ir t ______________

Circle the correct word.

1

letter	dirt

2

soccer	purse

3

turtle	skirt

4

shirt	letter

5
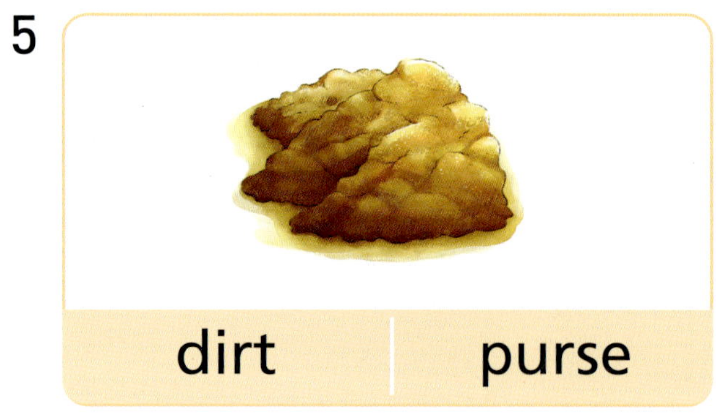

dirt	purse

6
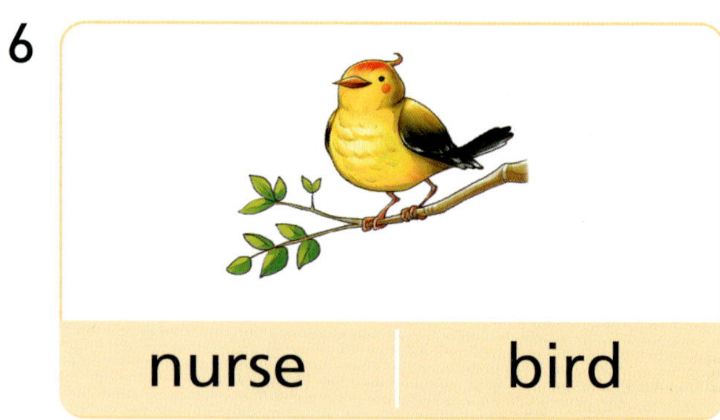

nurse	bird

7

skirt	flower

8
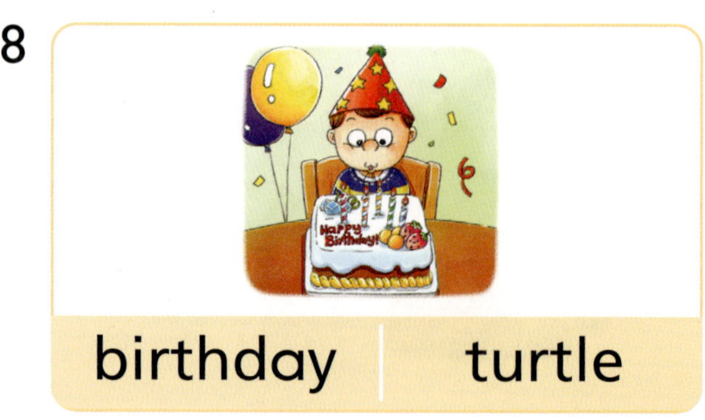

birthday	turtle

Write the word.

er

ur

ir

Circle the picture with the same vowel letters as the first picture.

1    

2    

3    

4    

5    

Circle the correct word for the picture.

1 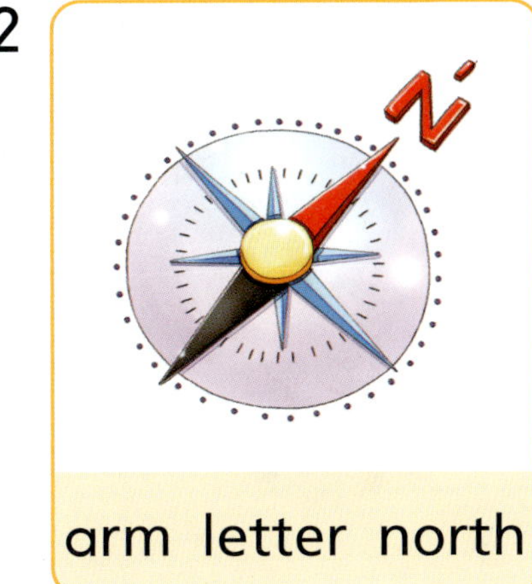
star fork soccer

2 
arm letter north

3 
shark girl corn

4 
horn purse park

5 
store bird turtle

6 
flower dirt nurse

7 
shirt horse card

8 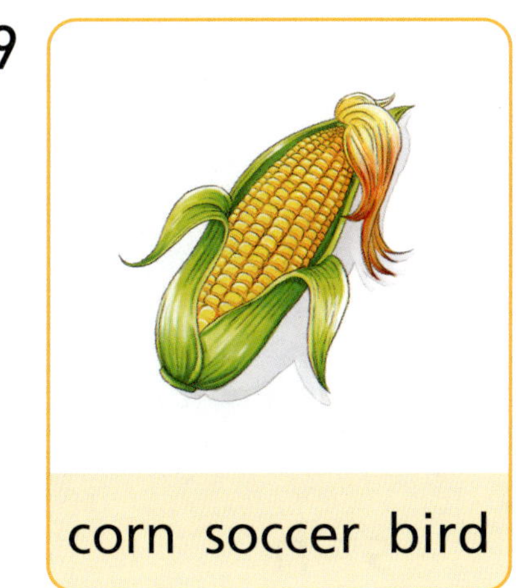
turtle skirt park

9
corn soccer bird

Choose and write the correct letters for the picture.

ar   ur   ir   or   er

1) f □ □ m e r   2) h □ □ s e   3) b □ □ d

4) n □ □ s e   5) l e t t □ □   6) □ □ m

7) s h □ □ t   8) h □ □ n   9) s t □ □ e

Find and circle. Then write the word.

s	o	c	c	e	r
k	o	a	w	g	r
i	a	r	m	i	o
r	i	d	i	r	t
t	u	r	t	l	e
s	t	o	r	e	d

1

____

2

____

3

____

4

____

5

____

6

____

7
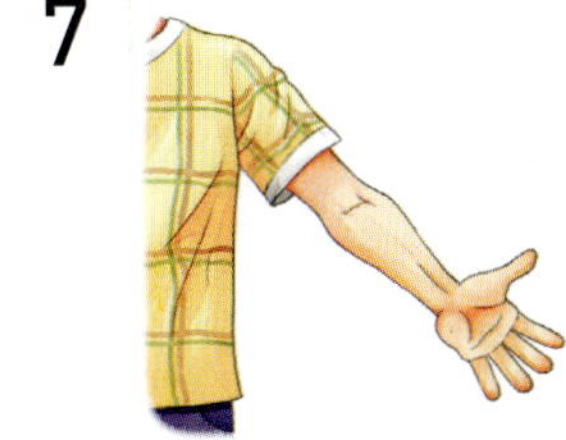
____

8

____

A

G

B

D

I

M

J

H

U

R

E

Phonics
wonder
LEVEL
5
Double Letter Vowels